SO, YOU WANT

To Work with the

ANCIENT AND

RECENT DEAD?

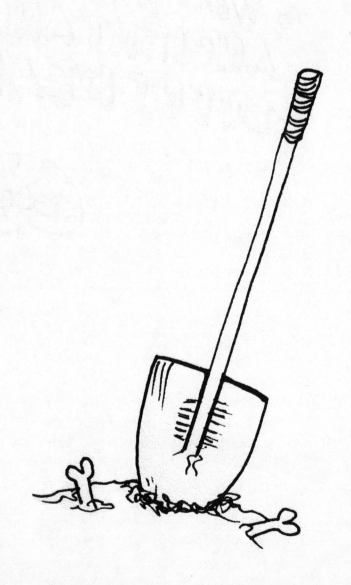

SO, YOU WANT

To Work with the ANCIENT AND RECENT DEAD?

Unearthing Careers from PALEONTOLOGY to FORENSIC SCIENCE

J. M. Bedell

BE WHAT YOU WANT Series

ALADDIN
New York London Toronto Sydney New Delhi

BEYOND WORDS
Hillsboro, Oregon

ALADDIN
An imprint of Simon & Schuster
Children's Publishing Division
1230 Avenue of the Americas
New York, NY 10020

BEYOND WORDS
20827 N.W. Cornell Road, Suite 500
Hillsboro, Oregon 97124-9808
503-531-8700 / 503-531-8773 fax
www.beyondword.com

This Beyond Words/Aladdin edition October 2015
Text copyright © 2015 by Beyond Words/Simon & Schuster, Inc.
Cover copyright © 2015 by Beyond Words/Simon & Schuster, Inc.
Interior illustrations copyright © 2015 by iStockphoto.com
Front cover photo copyright © 2015 by iStockphoto.com
Back cover photo copyright © 2015 by Randy Faris/Corbis

ALADDIN is a trademark of Simon & Schuster, Inc., and related logo is a registered trademark of Simon & Schuster, Inc.
Beyond Words is an imprint of Simon & Schuster, Inc. and the Beyond Words logo is a registered trademark of Beyond Words Publishing, Inc.

For information about special discounts for bulk purchases, please contact Simon & Schuster Special Sales at 1-866-506-1949 or business@simonandschuster.com.

The Simon & Schuster Speakers Bureau can bring authors to your live event. For more information or to book an event contact the Simon & Schuster Speakers Bureau at 1-866-248-3049 or visit our website at www.simonspeakers.com.

Managing Editor: Lindsay S. Brown
Design: Sara E. Blum
The text of this book was set in Bembo and Interstate.

Manufactured in the United States of America 1015 FFG

10 9 8 7 6 5 4 3 2 1

Library of Congress Cataloging-in-Publication Data

Bedell, J. M. (Jane M.).
  So, you want to work with the ancient and recent dead? : unearthing careers from
    paleontology to forensic science / by J. M. Bedell.
    pages cm. — (Be what you want series)
  1. Forensic sciences—Vocational guidance—Juvenile literature. 2. Forensic
    anthropology—Vocational guidance—Juvenile literature. 3. Archaeology—
    Vocational guidance—Juvenile literature. 4. Paleontology—Vocational
    guidance—Juvenile literature. I. Title. II. Series: Be what you want series.
HV8073.8.B44 2015
331.702—dc23

               2014047433

ISBN 978-1-58270-546-0 (hc)
ISBN 978-1-58270-545-3 (pbk)
ISBN 978-1-4814-3846-9 (eBook)

Always there has been an adventure just around the corner—and the world is still full of corners!

—Roy Chapman Andrews, archaeologist

CONTENTS

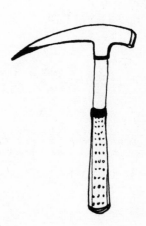

1

Choosing a Career Working with the Dead

Choosing to work with the dead can begin with a fascination with zombies, murder mysteries, or the heavy metal band Lordi. You may be captivated by the macabre, enchanted by ghost stories, or think your Goth lifestyle is a predictor of your future vocation. But choosing a career working with the dead takes some thought and a lot of planning. There are many ways to work with the dead, and a careful review of the careers in this book will help guide you toward the one that's right for you—or it will help you decide that you'd rather be an accountant or a lawyer!

Reasons You May Want to Work with the Dead

A Passion for Helping Others

Is "organ donor" checked on your driver's license? Do you get teary eyed when you see someone is hurting? Are you the one who likes to organize food drives, mentor younger kids, or collect signatures on a petition to save the spotted owl? If you have a compassionate heart, then working as a funeral director, as a transplant surgeon, or in one of the many organizations that try to save animals from extinction may be the perfect career for you.

A Passion for Justice

Does the idea of a criminal getting away with murder make your blood boil? Does knowing that animals are going extinct every day make you want to scream, "Protect them for *my* grandkids too!"? Are you a passionate person? If you see injustice and are willing to fight to the bitter end to make things better, then consider a career as a forensic pathologist, coroner, or phylogeneticist.

A Passion for the "Dead" Arts

Do graveyards, ghosts, and cemeteries fill you with wonder? Does pale skin and a vacant stare make you giddy? Do your fingers itch to paint a ghastly scene or write a story about a poltergeist? Is trying to look dead your daily challenge? Is your favorite color black? If you have an artistic bent, but it leans toward the macabre, then finding a career in the "dead" arts may be right for you.

A Passion for Discovery

Does an unsolved mystery keep you awake at night? Are you irritated when the pieces of a puzzle don't fit together properly? When you discover something new, does it fill you with glee? Does your mind seem to focus on finding better ways to use everyday items? If any of these questions pique your interest, consider a career as a paleontologist, aviation archaeologist, or thanatologist. There are many careers working with the dead where you can unravel a mystery, solve a crime, or even rewrite history.

A Passion for the Past

Would you rub your hands with delight at the thought of spending weeks digging in the dirt? Do you imagine yourself fighting on ancient battlefields, sailing across uncharted seas, or walking in the footsteps of prehistoric man? Does the idea of living when the pyramids or the Great Wall of China were being built send chills down your spine? If you answered yes to any of these questions, then a career as an archaeologist may be right for you. You may also want to consider working as a historian, as a history teacher, or in myriad other careers where you can study the past.

A Passion for Mess, Blood, and Gore

Do you run to biology class so you can be the first to dissect a frog? Does the smell of formaldehyde make you think, *This is gonna be interesting*? Are you okay with the sight of blood, the smell of rotting meat, the thought of touching something dead, and the idea of handling bodily fluids? If you see yourself saying yes to any of these questions, then you should look into working as a funeral director, a taxidermist, or an embalmer.

As you start thinking about a career working with the dead, it's important that you understand that many of these jobs will require a lot from you. It's not easy talking to a woman who just lost her child, working in the desert under a blazing hot sun, or digging through stacks and stacks of paper to find one interesting fact or clue that will help you find an ancestor or solve a crime.

The dead will demand that you study hard, work hard, think deeply, and care passionately. The toll that some of these jobs can take on your time and your emotions can be overwhelming. But if you find a career you love, you will be rewarded over and over again.

Look around. When you are ready to investigate a career, there will be others who have traveled the path you want to take and who are ready and willing, even excited, to give you a helping hand. All you have to do is ask.

WORKING STIFF *profile*

JAMES P. DELGADO
DIRECTOR OF MARITIME HERITAGE FOR NOAA's OFFICE OF
NATIONAL MARINE SANCTUARIES
SILVER SPRING, MARYLAND

When did you first become interested in archaeology and decide to make marine archaeology the focus of your career?

I learned about archaeology in the fifth and sixth grades in school. Then when I discovered that there was a three-thousand-year-old Ohlone Indian site in my hometown that was about to be bulldozed, it led me, at the age of fourteen, to try to rescue it from the bulldozers. I worked with my copy of *The Amateur Archaeologist's Handbook*, met with archaeologists, and lobbied my town's mayor to protect that archaeological site. I remained fascinated by and worked with archaeology on land until 1978 and the discovery of a buried ship in downtown San Francisco. My work for the National Park Service (NPS) on that site led me to ships, shipwrecks, and the fascinating world of underwater archaeology.

What education/work path did you take to get where you are today?

My educational path in terms of standard milestones was a BA, an MA, and finally a PhD. Life, experience in the field, and patient mentoring taught me much more.

At age twenty, I found myself one afternoon standing in the heart of the financial district in San Francisco. There, in the middle of a huge construction hole, I saw the black-stained bones of the whale ship *Niantic*. I stared, transfixed, at this relic of San Francisco's Gold Rush, unearthed amidst high-rises after a 129-year slumber beneath the landfill that buried the old waterfront.

The discovery of the whaler *Lydia*, a few months after *Niantic's* accidental resurrection, and the February 1979 excavation of another Gold Rush ship, the *William Gray*, at the base of Telegraph Hill, firmly set the course of my career.

I joined the cultural resources management team at the Golden Gate National Recreation Area (GGNRA) as park historian. The GGNRA was then a 36,000-acre national park, primarily intended to provide natural, cultural, recreational, and aesthetic areas for the people of the city and visitors. My nine years in San Francisco were an intensive lesson in the documentation and preservation of historic and archaeological sites in the park.

I also began to work outside of GGNRA, thanks to the NPS's growing awareness of a vast array of shipwrecks within the boundaries of our national parks, including the SS *Winfield Scott*. Diving on the "Winnie" added to my understanding of the first steamers to navigate the Pacific coast, and reminded me of the importance of the Gold Rush to the early history of California's development.

From Drakes Bay to the warm waters of Pearl Harbor and the battle-ravaged remains of the USS *Arizona*, to a wreck at the turbulent mouth of the Columbia River, to the atomic-bombed fleet at Bikini Atoll, with interludes in Cape Cod and back home at GGNRA, I was taught how to dive wrecks and how to "do" underwater archaeology.

I took a sabbatical from the NPS and earned my master's degree at East Carolina University. I enrolled in a relatively

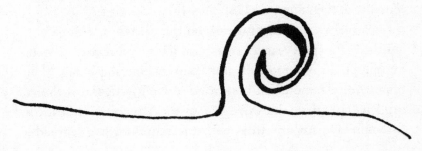

new program in Maritime History and Underwater Research, which was one of only two programs in the United States to offer a graduate degree.

Just before I left North Carolina, I got a phone call from Edwin C. "Ed" Bearss, the chief historian of the NPS. He asked if I would like to join an NPS team to help the National Oceanic and Atmospheric Administration (NOAA) manage the wreck of the USS *Monitor*. I served as the project's historian for the next few years, writing the study that made the wreck a National Historic Landmark. Assessing *Monitor*, a famous icon shipwreck, was a revealing look at why people think certain things are historic and worth saving.

In early 1987, Ed Bearss asked me to run a new program for the NPS, the National Maritime Initiative (NMI). A large part of my job was to create a national maritime preservation program for the US government, inventorying every known historic maritime resource, from floating ships and shipwrecks to lighthouses and shipyards. I spent nine months of each year in the field, visiting almost every one of our nation's 330 historic ships, climbing hundreds of lighthouse towers, visiting shipyards and naval facilities, and diving down to see underwater wrecks.

My time in the NPS also included summer shipwreck expeditions, which included dives to the storm-ravaged square-rigger *Avanti* at Fort Jefferson, Florida, and to the USS *Arizona* and USS *Utah* at Pearl Harbor, Hawaii, where we also searched for crashed Japanese aircraft and sunken midget submarines from the December 5, 1941, attack. I spent my last field season in 1990 leading a team to Mexico to study the remains of the 1846 brig USS *Somers*.

In early 1991, when my work on the NMI was complete, I left the NPS. The years of travel had left me yearning to focus on one place, one museum, one ship, or one shipwreck. The opportunity came when I returned to the Pacific Coast to live in Canada and work as director of the Vancouver Maritime Museum. During my time with the museum, I've learned a

lot, especially while working on television documentaries
fascinating wrecks of the undersea world are a great mus
and I've had the privilege of sitting in a front row seat to some
amazing displays and galleries.

**You have worked on over a hundred shipwrecks. What
fascinates you about this work, and why is it important?**
Shipwrecks fascinate me on many levels. They focus on moments
in time, and act as symbols or icons. They give us the opportunity to reflect on human nature. They allow us, as a society, to
discuss how we will deal with them—as objects to be salvaged,
as memorials to the dead, as historic sites worthy of preservation. Shipwrecks remind me of why I am an archaeologist: to
study people through what they do and what they leave behind.

Why the work is important has many answers—for science,
for education, for inspiration. We need to use shipwrecks as
a way to focus attention on our oceans, seas, and lakes, to
recognize that they are a vital part of this planet. We must
understand, conserve, and nurture them, and in doing so,
ensure our own survival.

**Describe your work as the executive director of the
Vancouver Maritime Museum.**
For fifteen years, I worked with a great team at the
museum. We organized a three-million-dollar reenactment
of the historic Northwest Passage and North America-
circumnavigating voyages of the museum's
centerpiece exhibit, the Royal Canadian
Mounted Police schooner *St. Roch*. Serving
as a member of the crew of the *St. Roch
II*'s Voyage of Rediscovery meant visiting
Arctic ports and connecting with people who
remembered the original ship and its crew.

We rescued and reconstructed the *Ben Franklin*,
a historic oceanographic research submersible PX-15.
Restoring *Ben Franklin* meant working with crane operators and

volunteers to reassemble the sub a piece at a time, bolting and hammering two stories up, hoping to God that I didn't fall!

Since the museum is small, I had the freedom to work hands-on with the research, the exhibits, the visitor programs, and the projects. What I learned was that museums are not only repositories of things—they are places where society gathers its collective memories and preserves what it holds dear.

For a time, you were host and team archaeologist for the National Geographic television series _The Sea Hunters_. Describe your tenure there and what you learned from that experience.

I spent six years working in documentary television with producer John Davis; cohost, novelist, storyteller, and shipwreck-hunter Clive Cussler; master divers Mike and Warren Fletcher; and a great behind-the-camera crew. We traveled the globe, meeting other divers, diving to amazing wrecks, and sharing stories with millions of viewers around the world.

I learned from that experience that people of all walks of life are fascinated with shipwrecks and history. _The Sea Hunters_ reached a lot of folks. It reminded me that what I deal with as a scholar means very little if my intended audience is a handful of fellow academics. My work has to be relevant and accessible to everyone. As scientists, we need to welcome interest, questions, and participation.

As director of Maritime Heritage, describe your work for this government organization and why it is important.

The National Marine Sanctuaries are a precious part of America's cultural and natural legacy. Today, I am a part of a team that is focused on conserving our oceans by educating people about their importance. We use not only shipwrecks, but also the ongoing story of how and why we as people have interacted with the sea. We emphasize how it has changed us, and how now, increasingly, and not in a good way, we are changing it.

We need sanctuaries. We need to preserve them. And we need more attention paid to the 71 percent of the planet that defines not only our past but also our future.

What is the most exciting excavation you've worked on, and why was it important to you?
You know what? They've all been exciting. It's not the most famous, the deepest, the oldest, the most artifact laden, or the most challenging ones. It's the collective sense of all of them that speaks to human nature—to our ingenuity, stupidity, enterprise, greed, self-sacrifice, bravery, cowardice, and all other aspects of who we are as humans. My most exciting projects are the ones that have yet to happen. The most exciting are the ones I get to share with as many people as I can.

What advice would you give a young person who is interested in becoming a marine archaeologist?
Focus on all aspects of archaeology, not just marine archaeology, to expand your horizons and your opportunities. Not all that is amazing is beneath the sea, but a great deal of it is. Find your passion for the past wherever you can. Understand that your career will unfold built on how well you work with others, how much you are willing to share, and how hard you work. Remember, all good things take time. Study hard. Know your math, science, and engineering. Learn art and literature. Learn to write and speak well, and never shy away from showing that you care and are passionate about your work.

What do you see as future trends in marine archaeology?
I see amazing new trends in surveying and documenting wrecks with higher resolution sonars, lasers, and low-light camera systems. New robotic technologies will ultimately survey the 95 percent of the ocean floor that remains unknown. The most important trend, however, is going to be internet driven. Remote access and live interaction technology will

allow everyone to go along on the adventure, exploring, learning, and contributing as citizen scientists—or just asking questions—as we go out into the final frontier, the oceans, in search of new life and past civilization.

SUPERMASSIVE DINOSAUR FOUND IN ARGENTINA!

Its name is *Dreadnoughtus schrani*, and it was a dreadfully scary creature! Scientists have over 70 percent of its bones, so they know about how big it really was. At 85 feet (26 meters) long and weighing in at about 65 tons (59,300 kilograms), it is the largest land animal ever known to exist, and scientists say it died before it was fully grown. Other supermassive dinosaurs have had their measurements calculated based on only a few pieces, but this one is awesome because it is so complete; it gives scientists a chance to understand dinosaur anatomy and muscle structure. Unfortunately, its skull is missing.

Should You Work With the Dead? Quiz

1. I would describe myself as
A. organized, compassionate, hardworking
B. passionate, determined, someone who fights for the underdog
C. unique, quiet, artistic, thoughtful
D. inquisitive, inventive, a problem solver
E. adventurous, someone who likes to get dirty, a role player
F. friendly, never grossed out, helpful

2. My friends and family think I am
  A. the one who always tries to help
  B. the one with a strong sense of right and wrong
  C. the one who thinks and feels deeply
  D. the one who searches for the right answer
  E. the one who is active, a doer
  F. the one who loves disgusting things

3. If I knew I was going to die tomorrow, I'd spend my last day
  A. comforting my family and friends
  B. protesting that I am too young and demanding another opinion
  C. writing a poem or essay or painting a picture to share at my funeral
  D. researching ways to extend my life
  E. having as many adventures as possible
  F. touring the morgue to see what dead bodies look like

4. If I had to write a research paper, my topic would be
  A. how to organize a "Save the Whales" campaign
  B. how to change opinions or pass new laws
  C. how to write a poem or essay
  D. defining the main characteristics of an inventor
  E. how to write a role-playing game
  F. alternate uses for blood, guts, and gore

5. My favorite movies or television shows are
  A. cartoons, romance, happy-ending movies
  B. crime dramas or spy thrillers
  C. independent films
  D. mystery or science fiction
  E. historical biopics or adventure
  F. horror

6. When I've had a long day, I relax by
   A. organizing an outing with friends
   B. going door-to-door collecting clothes for the homeless
   C. lying in bed and writing in my journal
   D. heading to the kitchen to create a new recipe
   E. going for a run
   F. cleaning cages at the animal shelter

7. If I was at the park and a little kid fell and started crying, I would
   A. rush to the child, yelling, "Oh no! Are you hurt?"
   B. approach the parents and scold them for not paying attention
   C. watch to see what happens so I can write about it later
   D. look for ways to make the park a safer place to play
   E. sit down next to the child and start digging in the dirt
   F. immediately go and clean up the blood

If you answered mostly
A: Consider a career as a grief counselor, transplant surgeon, or death midwife.
B: Consider a career as a forensic pathologist, coroner, or phylogeneticist.
C: Consider a career as an artist, an obituary writer, or a monument designer.
D: Consider a career as a paleontologist, an aviation archaeologist, or a thanatologist.
E: Consider a career as an archaeologist, a logger, or a ghost hunter.
F: Consider a career as a funeral director, taxidermist, or embalmer.

2

Discovering the Ancient Dead: Humans and Civilizations

How long have humans lived on the earth? No one knows for sure, but archaeologists around the world are looking for the answer. They are searching everywhere for clues, pieces to a puzzle that will one day reveal a timeline that maps our species's transformation into the humans we are today.

Where did early humans live? How did they survive? When did they begin to live in groups? What was it like to live a million years ago? A thousand years ago? These and many other questions are asked every day by archaeologists who are curious about how people lived in every era of human existence.

ANTHROPOLOGY AND ARCHAEOLOGY

Anthropology is the study of humans and civilizations throughout time, including those who live today. *Archaeology* is a subset of anthropology because it is only the study of humans who lived long ago.

Archaeologists study ancient dead humans by finding and analyzing the things they left behind like bones, tools, pottery, buildings, poop, and written records. Human history is divided into two huge categories: *prehistoric*, which is the time before written language, and *historic*, which is the time after written language. When archaeologists date things, they use BCE, which means "before the Common Era" and CE, which means "Common Era." Our Gregorian calendar, which is used in most parts of the world, starts at 1 CE, and today we live in the twenty-first century CE.

Prehistoric time is divided into four periods named for the type of tools the people used. In different parts of the world, the dates of each era may be slightly different.

- **The Stone Age** lasted around 2.5 million years and ended around 6000 BCE to 4000 BCE. During this time period, humans used stones as their principle tools.

- **The Copper Age,** 3200 BCE to 2300 BCE, is when humans started using copper to make their tools.

- **The Bronze Age,** 2300 BCE to 700 BCE, is when humans began to use bronze for their tools.

- **The Iron Age,** 700 BCE to 1 BCE, is when humans began using iron and then steel for cutting tools and weapons.

Beginning with the first known human etchings on stone, *historical* time is divided into four periods. Written language developed independently in different areas of the world, but the oldest known *pictograms*, pictures used to mean words or phrases, are about five thousand years old.

- **Ancient history** begins around 3500 BCE in Mesopotamia and ends around 900 CE.

- **The post-classical era,** or the Middle Ages, dates from 500 CE to 1500 CE.

- **The early modern era** dates from 1500 CE to 1700 CE.

- **The modern era** dates from 1700 CE to today.

SURPRISE! SURPRISE! THOSE DATES THEY KEEP A CHANGIN'

In 1993, professor George Hourmouziadis and his team found a wooden tablet with written text on it, buried on a Greek island. The tablet has been dated to about 5260 BCE. Their discovery was announced in 2004 and calls into question the long-held belief that written language began around 800 BCE. The tablet was damaged when it was exposed to the oxygen-rich atmosphere and is undergoing preservation.

In 2013, etchings on stoneware were found in eastern China. They are about 1400 years older than the oracle bones, which have Chinese writing on them and date to the Shang dynasty, around 3600 years ago.

With each new discovery, the dates for the oldest written language change. This is the fun part about working as an archaeologist: you can actually change history!

Archaeologist

Working with the ancient dead can be very exciting! Especially if you get a chance to discover a new, previously unknown civilization, find a long-lost city, or uncover the remains of primitive people living in unexpected places.

FEDERAL HISTORIC PRESERVATION LEGISLATION

1906 Antiquities Act protects historic, prehistoric, and scientific features located on federal lands.

1966 US Historic Preservation Act protects and preserves property that is of historical significance. It created the National Register of Historic Places.

1969 National Environmental Policy Act preserves important historic, cultural, and natural aspects of our national heritage.

1974 Archaeological and Historic Preservation Act recovers and preserves historical and archaeological data that might be lost or destroyed in the construction of dams or reservoirs, including all activity related to the building of these sites.

1979 Archaeological Resources Protection Act defines "archaeological resources" as any material remains of past human life or activity that is of archaeological interest and is at least one hundred years old.

As an archaeologist, your career will focus on the study of past humans and the cultures in which they lived. From life in Africa a million years ago to life in America in the 1600s, archaeologists around the world are making new discoveries every day. Their discoveries, along with knowledge gleaned from the work of earlier archaeologists, are leading to newer and greater understanding of what life was like for the human race since our very beginning.

The job opportunities for an archaeologist are increasing. Why? Because federal and state legislators are passing laws that require the government to preserve and maintain sites that are of historical significance to all Americans or to the people who live in a region or state. It is called Cultural Resource Management (CRM), and archaeologists help developers and public agencies find the best ways to meet the requirements of these laws. CRM archaeologists find previously unknown sites and artifacts, evaluate the importance of the artifacts, and conduct rescue excavations if the remains are threatened by development.

A career as an archaeologist can be rewarding, but it will take a lot of studying to get there. The minimum amount of education you will need to work with ancient remains or on a historic site is a bachelor's degree with a major in anthropology or archaeology and some field training. Most students get their field training by attending summer archaeology field schools or volunteering at an archaeological site. There are few job opportunities outside the United States for those with only a bachelor's degree.

After you get a bachelor's degree, you can continue your studies by getting a master's degree. A master's degree will allow you to work in the private sector or in a museum, and you can teach at a community college. It is also enough education for most government positions.

A doctoral degree requires another two to three years of study. With this degree, you can teach at a college or university, become a museum curator, or be the lead investigator on an archaeological dig. It is important to note that most foreign governments will not issue an excavation permit to anyone without a doctoral degree. Without one, you will probably be working only on digs within the United States.

Archaeologists focus their careers on a specific time period, like the Islamic Golden Age (700–1300 CE), or in a certain specialty, like finding and documenting shipwrecks. Choosing your area will depend on what interests you most. Some students major in archaeological studies as a broad-based liberal arts major which allows them to enter careers in business, communications, medicine, or law. Other students choose programs that combine archaeology with another discipline, like Greek and Roman history, a foreign language, art, or architecture.

Ten Areas of Archaeological Study

1. **Archaeoastronomy** is the study of how ancient people studied the stars, to understand how they learned and developed their calendar systems and remembered celestial events. This includes the study of celestial myths and legends, religions, and the worldviews of ancient cultures.

2. **Archaeology by culture** is when a lot of work is done in a specific region. That group of archaeologists get a category of their own. Here are a few:

   African archaeology—study of ancient societies in Africa

   American archaeology—study of ancient societies in North and South America

   classical archaeology—study of past societies in the Mediterranean region, mainly Roman and Greek

   Egyptology—study of ancient societies in Egypt

   medieval archaeology—study of the medieval period in Europe

   Near Eastern archaeology—study of the area between Modern Europe and Modern Iraq (the Fertile Crescent)

3. **Aviation archaeology** is the study and preservation of old aircraft crash sites.

4. **Battlefield archaeology** is the study and preservation of documented battlefields and undocumented areas of conflict. This field focuses on trying to determine what actually happened without focusing on the cause of the conflict.

5. **Economic archaeology** is the study of the relationship between ancient people and their natural and cultural resources.

6. **Industrial archaeology** is the study of historically significant industrial sites, structures, artifacts, and technology.

7. **Maritime (marine) archaeology** is the study of human interactions with bodies of water by studying submerged landscapes, human remains, shipwrecks, and other related structures and artifacts.

8. **Prehistoric archaeology and historic archaeology** are studies of cultures and people in the time before written language and the time after written language.

9. **Public archaeology** is the practice of sharing archaeological findings with the public and promoting the preservation and management of historical sites. People who work in this area try to make archaeology relevant to everyone through lectures, books, museum displays, and opening archaeological sites to the public.

10. **Urban archaeology** is the study of towns and cities where humans have lived for a long time and where there is a huge record of the past.

WORKING STIFF *profile*

LISA M. DALY, AVIATION ARCHAEOLOGIST
ARCHAEOLOGY PhD CANDIDATE, MEMORIAL UNIVERSITY OF NEWFOUNDLAND
ST. JOHN'S, NEWFOUNDLAND AND LABRADOR, CANADA

When did you first become interested in aviation archaeology and decide to make it the focus of your career?

I first became interested in aviation archaeology while working on an aviation site. I had just returned home after completing a master of science in forensic and biological anthropology at Bournemouth University in the UK, and I was looking for an archaeology job.

The project I worked on was a survey and excavation of a United States Army Air Force B-24 that crashed on February 14, 1945, near Gander, Newfoundland. There were ten men on board, and all perished in the crash. What I found interesting, and what made me want to work in this field, was finding the personal effects of those who were on the aircraft. The buttons from their clothing, the pins from their lapels, the razors they used for shaving, their bottle opener for opening soda—those items revealed to me the men on that aircraft who gave their lives for the war effort.

What education/work path did you take to get where you are today?

As a teenager, I was always interested in English and biology. I knew when I went to university that I wanted to study biology. In my second year, I took an anthropology course, and in the first class, the professor introduced the four branches of anthropology: social cultural anthropology, linguistics, archaeology, and biological or physical anthropology. When he described physical anthropology, I knew that was what I wanted to study. The study of physical anthropology included everything that I found interesting about biology, with the added cultural studies that I enjoyed. In my biology courses, I always found genetics interesting and learned I could do genetic research as part of physical anthropology. I graduated from Memorial University of Newfoundland, and went to Bournemouth University in the United Kingdom to do a master of science in forensic and biological anthropology. For my MS dissertation, I attempted to recover mitochondrial deoxyribonucleic acid (mtDNA) from ancient cremated human remains, allowing me to combine many of the areas of study I was interested in.

What is the process you use to locate and document a historic crash site?

When I decide on a historic crash site to research, I contact a number of people who have visited or done some research on that site. They often give me a good idea of where the site is located. Sometimes, people contact me because they found a site, and I will talk to my colleagues and see if we can identify the aircraft. If I can, I try to get the crash or incident report before visiting the site.

Before any site visit, I secure a permit from the Provincial Archaeology Office of Newfoundland and Labrador. All archaeological work in this province requires a permit and requires archaeologists to follow a set of regulations for any archaeological research. There is often a lot of trial and error to find the aircraft crash sites that remain around Newfoundland and Labrador because they are generally in very isolated locations. Once I locate a site, I set up my survey equipment, a handheld GPS, a surveyor's level, and a tape measure. I establish a datum, a point on the site that everything will be measured in reference to, and I record all of the fragments of aircraft found on the site. For sites with large pieces, wings or sections of fuselage, I take multiple measurements. These measurements are used to create a map of the site which might give an idea of how the aircraft crashed.

I take pictures of everything on site. In rare situations, if there are artifacts of historical significance, I collect them and bring them back to the laboratory for conservation. My priority is to create an inventory of what remains on site and to create a map of the site to complement the historical record. Then I have to write a report to submit to the Provincial Archaeology Office of Newfoundland and Labrador. If I can, I also try to present my research to the community.

What fascinates you about locating old crash sites?
The thrill of discovery—then, after a closer look, the story that the site can tell. These sites are important for a few different reasons. First, they tell the history of World War II in Newfoundland and Labrador, and in North America. These aircraft belonged to the United States Army Air Force, the Royal Air Force (Britain), and the Royal Canadian Air Force. In some cases, there were fatalities in the plane crashes, and it is important to remember those who gave the ultimate sacrifice in the war effort.

How does an airplane crash site differ from other archaeological sites?
Crash sites differ because much of the wreckage is found on the surface, so there is typically little excavation. The work tends to be more about surveying instead of excavating. Also, the regulations for most archaeological sites in Newfoundland and Labrador say that everything needs to be collected and conserved. In the case of airplane crash sites, the regulations are a little different, and most of the site can be left undisturbed, just surveyed.

Also, crash sites are more modern sites; thus, there are many different types of materials on them, often as part of a single artifact. For instance, one piece of machinery may contain aluminum, copper, porcelain, plastic, and rubber, all of which must be cleaned and conserved differently.

Can you explain conflict archaeology and why it interests you?
Conflict archaeology is the study of the material remains of human conflict. That can mean war plane crash sites, the buildings and structures associated with military, naval, and air bases, the sites of battles—anything associated with war and conflict.

I find it to be an interesting area of research because periods of conflict, especially modern conflict, have done

so much to create the world
we live in, and it is important
to remember and honor those
who fought and worked in
those conflicts.

**What is the most exciting
excavation you've worked
on, and why was it impor-
tant to you?**

That most exciting excavation
I've worked on was my first aviation site. It was the United
States Army Air Force B-24 (mentioned above) which crashed
during a snowstorm. It was a high-energy crash, and the
debris spread over a large area of land. It took over two weeks
to survey the site, and it was not until all of the documents
were read and the map analyzed that the site could be properly
understood and we got a good idea of what happened.

Taking this information and sharing it with the pilot's son
made the site that much more important to me. Mr. Dolan
always had questions as to what happened to his father, Colonel Dolan, and what happened to the aircraft. Mr. Dolan came
to Newfoundland to see the site, and when he left, he had a
much better understanding of what happened to his father so
many years ago. It was very rewarding to know that I could
do work that was so important to someone else.

**What advice would you give a young person who is
interested in becoming an aviation archaeologist?**

If you are interested in aviation archaeology, you need to have
a good circle of colleagues to ask advice and bounce ideas off
of. You also need to work with the communities associated
with the crash sites. In Newfoundland and Labrador, they are
very interested in their own history and support archaeological
research. Otherwise, make sure to research the sites and any
legislation that may apply. There are different international

regulations that can apply to airplane crash sites, and researchers need to make sure they work within those regulations and know the laws.

If you are really interested in aviation archaeology, do some research and see who is working in that field and if they need volunteers. Working on a site will really tell you if it is the career path for you.

What do you see as future trends in aviation archaeology?
Aviation archaeology is in its infancy. I see better research methods being developed as more sites are studied and better equipment becomes available. As more sites are investigated, academics and the public will gain a better understanding of what aviation archaeological material remains on the landscape. And better laws will be developed to protect these sites. More research will also help tell the story of each aircraft, each aircrew, and all of the people who helped in the war effort.

WHERE ARCHAEOLOGISTS WORK

- Archaeology centers
- Colleges and universities
- Consulting firms
- County and city governments
- Cultural resource management companies
- Federal government (Bureau of Land Management, US Army Corps of Engineers, National Park Service, US Bureau of Reclamation, US Fish and Wildlife Service, and the US Forest Service)
- Historical societies

- Museums

- Private corporations

- Research organizations

- State historic preservation offices; departments of conservation, natural resources, and transportation; and state parks and recreation

FATHERS OF ARCHAEOLOGY

Ciriaco de'Pizzicolli (1391-1452) was one of the first to study the ancient ruins of Greece and Rome. He recorded where they were located and their current condition. He understood their importance to future generations and tried to get the local authorities to protect and preserve them.

Flavio Biondo (1392-1463) was an Italian historian who created guides to the crumbling ruins of Rome.

Niccolò Marcello Venuti (1700-1755) was employed by King Charles of Naples and Sicily to excavate the ancient city of Herculaneum. His excavation is considered the first modern archaeological dig because he used a careful and methodical approach to his work.

Thomas Jefferson (1743-1826) was an American president and historian. Around 1781, he carefully excavated a Native American burial mound on his property by cutting a wedge out of it and then examining and documenting the layers of soil and the artifacts he found. This method of excavation was ahead of its time and earns him a place on the list of early archaeologists.

Working as an Archaeologist

Archaeologists are interested in ancient people. They want to understand who they were, where they lived, and how they survived. No matter what culture an archaeologist chooses to study, the main goals are to gather information and try to piece together what everyday life was like many, many years ago.

Although there are many areas of study, most archaeologists conduct field investigations, analyze what they find, and publish the results of their research. Beyond that, some also focus on teaching future archaeologists and educating the public about the need to preserve artifacts and historical sites.

Every archaeologist starts out as a "shovel bum," or entry-level field technician. From there, you work your way up to a crew chief and then to principle investigator. Along the way, you will get sweaty, dirty, and tired. You will dig in the dirt, sift through debris, get bitten by bugs, and run away from snakes, scorpions, and maybe even a bear or cougar. And you will call all of this FUN!

Skills and Qualities of an Archaeologist

- Ability to draw maps and take photographs

- Accurate reporting and recording skills

- An inquisitive and analytical mind

- Attention to detail

- Computer skills

- Good time management

- Likes to work on a team

- Physically fit and enthusiastic
- Patient
- Willing to work in various locations

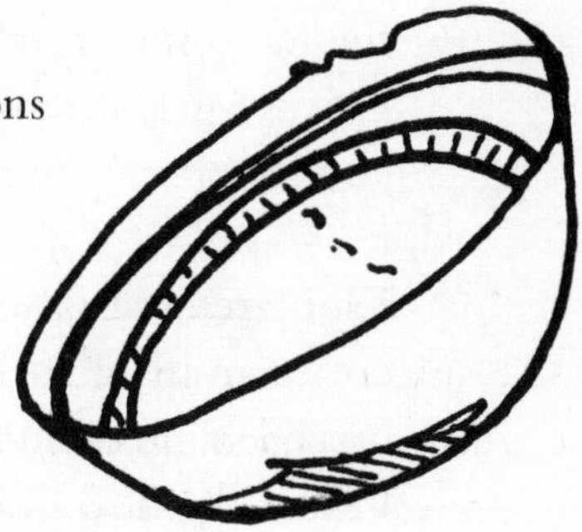

Choosing a Site

In the past, an archaeological dig could last for years and encompass huge areas of land. Today, because of the high cost of excavation and concern for preserving the archaeological record, most digs last a short time and cover as small an area as possible.

Before a shovel ever touches the ground, archaeologists have already done their homework. They know what they are looking for (a fort, a wall, a burial site) and where they will probably find it (near a river, in a valley, inside a cave). After careful review of all the available written information, like maps, deeds, and census and tax records, or after conducting a field survey, an excavation site is carefully chosen.

AFRICA: THE CRADLE OF MANKIND

In East Africa, at a place called Oldupai Gorge (originally misnamed Olduvai), archaeologists Louis and Mary Leakey found some of our earliest ancestors buried beneath layers of sediment. The oldest of the four remains found was named "Nutcracker Man," and he lived about 1.75 million years ago.

Knowing exactly where to dig is important. Depending on the terrain, an archaeologist can use one or more of the following to narrow down a large area to a small, specific spot.

- **Ground-penetrating radar** uses radar pulses to create an image of what is underground. This radar is electromagnetic radiation in the microwave bandwidth of the radio spectrum. Microwaves are also used in spacecraft communication and much of the world's data, television, and telephone communications.

- **Electrical resistance meters** use electrical pulses to create an image of what is underground. For example, a buried stone building can be mapped because the walls hinder the flow of electricity, but the soil inside or outside the wall will conduct it more easily.

- **Magnetometers** measure the earth's magnetic field to create an image of what is either underground or underwater. There are several types, but they all help to detect things like buried baked bricks, compacted ancient roads, or submerged shipwrecks.

- **Metal detectors** use electricity to create an electromagnetic field that can detect metal objects buried underground. When the unit crosses over or near a metal object, it transmits a signal that is then transmitted into an earpiece or displayed on a meter. Handheld metal detectors are common, but more sensitive ones mounted on wheeled carts are sometimes used.

- **Light detection and ranging (LIDAR)** uses light, often pulses from a laser, to measure distances. Different materials reflect light at varying speeds and scatter it in different ways. This light is then absorbed by the sensors and interpreted by computers to create an image. LIDAR is used to map features hidden under the canopy of trees, reveal features that cannot be seen from the ground, and create elevation models of sites that are hidden by vegetation.

♀ **Aerial photography** is used to take pictures from the International Space Station, satellites, airplanes, drones, and even kites. When a picture is taken from directly overhead or from an angle, it can reveal ancient ruins, roads, or waterways. They can also be combined to create three-dimensional pictures of a site. Aerial photography can detect shadow marks that show slight differences in ground levels, crop marks that are tone or color differences on the ground that may define buried features, frost marks that reveal areas where water has accumulated against a buried feature, or soil marks that show up as slight differences in the color of the soil, which can reveal natural deposits or manmade features. Pictures taken before and after a heavy rain can also reveal features not seen from ground level.

♀ **Radio detection and ranging (RADAR)** uses pulses of microwave electromagnetic radiation to measure distance. These measurements are then used to create an image that shows all the variations in the earth's surface. Radar is often combined with infrared photography to detect small differences in ground temperatures that may lead to hidden sites. Sideways-looking radar (SLAR) is used to locate sites under the rainforest canopy.

FIRST AERIAL PHOTOGRAPHS

In 1913, while working at the archaeological digs of Jebel Moya and Abu Geile in the Sudan, Henry Wellcome pioneered the use of aerial photography. He used a camera attached to a box kite to take pictures of the surrounding terrain.

NAZCA LINES IN PERU

The Nazca Lines were first discovered by Peruvian archaeologist Toribio Mejía Xesspe in 1927 and date to around 700 BCE to 200 BCE. In the 1930s, the full extent of their beauty was realized when they were first seen and photographed from the air. The lines cross an area thirty-seven miles long and one mile wide. There are about nine hundred geometric forms—triangles, spirals, circles, trapezoids, and straight lines—and seventy animal and plant figures, including a spider, a monkey, a hummingbird, a killer whale, and a gigantic one-thousand-foot pelican.

ONE-THOUSAND-YEAR-OLD ROADS IN NEW MEXICO

In the spring of 1982, NASA found prehistoric roads, dating from 900 CE to 1000 CE, in Chaco Canyon, New Mexico. By using a Thermal Infrared Multispectral Scanner (TIMS), they were able to detect features that could not be seen by aerial photography or infrared imaging. After flying over the region three times, they discovered buildings, walls, crop fields, and over two hundred miles of roads.

Excavating a Site

Once a site is chosen, a detailed base map is created, showing exactly where the site is located and noting any previous excavation and artifact locations. Then the area is divided into a grid using survey equipment, string, and stakes. The grid is set with north, south, east, and west as the coordinates for the exterior lines. Inside that grid, string lines are placed in exact measurements of one foot or one meter, making a checkerboard pattern.

Now it's time for the field technicians to get to work. They examine each grid box, carefully removing layers of soil until they find an artifact. When a discovery is made, its exact location is recorded using the number of the square within the grid where the object was found.

Pictures are taken to document each step as the object is revealed. Carefully written, detailed notes describe the depth of soil the artifact was found in, the type of soil it was found in, and any other details about what surrounded it. Each artifact is carefully put in a bag that is labeled with the location, the excavator's name, and the soil layer in which it was found.

Working at an archaeological dig is backbreaking, meticulous work. It requires patience, stamina, and the ability to work as part of a team.

Excavation Tools

- **Box screen**—used to sift through dirt to find artifacts. The screen sits on a stand that allows the box to be shaken so fine particles fall through the mesh and larger artifacts remain on top. Nesting boxes with large to small mesh screens are used to sift out artifacts according to size.

- **Bucket auger**—used for testing deep soils, especially in floodplains. It can dig up to twenty-one feet (seven meters) into the ground.

- **Camera**—used to record how the dig and every artifact looked before, during, and after the excavation.

- **Caliper**—used to measure objects or the distance between two objects.

- **Coal scoop**—like a long-handled dustpan, it is used to remove debris from a site. Especially useful in square corners.

- **Cotton gloves**—used to keep the oil on your skin from damaging artifacts and to prevent cross-contamination of objects.

- **Drying rack**—clean artifacts are placed on racks to keep them safe and allow them to dry. Racks are used to organize artifacts according to where they are found.

- **Hand broom and dustpan**—used to delicately clean off dirt and rubble from the floor of a site, especially once archaeologists have begun using trowels instead of shovels.

- **Kneeling mat or kneepads**—used to protect knees from the hard ground.

- **Line level and plumb bob**—used to map a site and measure depth.

- **Magnifying glass**—used to see tiny objects up close.

- **Mattock**—a type of pickaxe used to break hard ground.

- **Notebook and pencil**—used to record every detail at a dig site. The paper and pens must be acid-free.

- **Scales**—used to weigh objects.

- **Shovel, rake, bucket, and wheelbarrow**—used to remove larger amounts of dirt.

- **Tape measures**—used to measure the depth of where an object was found, as well as to map a site.

- **Tongue depressor, toothpick, paintbrush, and spoon**—used to clean debris from artifacts and remove soil from tight spots.

- **Total station or transit**—tools that use global positioning system (GPS) technology, as well as longitude and latitude, to record exact heights and depths within a site and exactly where artifacts are found.

- **Trowel**—a small, flat-bladed tool used when shovels are too big.

SUCKING UP THE SEAFLOOR!

Marine archaeologists use similar tools, but when possible, they choose plastic versions to avoid rust. Instead of using shovels and buckets to remove large amounts of debris, they use a one-hundred-foot (30.5-meter) hose to suck up the seafloor sediment. A pump can move about six hundred gallons (2,271 liters) of water a minute and deposit the sediment into a box screen. The box has a fine mesh bottom that catches tiny artifacts and bits of bone.

Trash Can Challenge! *Activity*

Archaeologists can tell a lot about a society by what they threw away. Trash heaps, called *middens*, hold clues about a society's diet, wealth, population, and more. Archaeologists carefully excavate these middens and analyze the artifacts they find. In this activity, you are going to learn about a society in the same way—by analyzing your family's trash.

You can do this activity on your own, but getting two or three friends to join you will make it more fun and much more interesting. Remember to ask your parents for permission before you start this activity.

MATERIALS
1 large black trash bag
1 notebook
1 pen
disposable plastic gloves
1 plastic tarp or large plastic sheet
10–20 (1-gallon) clear plastic storage bags
1 permanent marker

STEP ONE: MUSTERING THE MIDDEN

Put the trash bag near your family's trash can. Ask each family member to put everything that isn't wet and smelly, like metal cans, plastic jugs, glass bottles, and cardboard boxes, as well as broken toys or electronics, into your bag. Dispose of everything else in the regular trash can.

Place your notebook and pen by your bag. For one week, record *everything* that is put in your bag. *And* on a separate sheet of paper, record *everything* that is put in the family trash (the wet and smelly stuff).

STEP TWO: DOCUMENTING THE DEBRIS

At the end of one week, take your bag of dry trash, note-book, pen, gloves, tarp, storage bags, and marker and meet up with your friends. Spread the tarp out on the ground and, one by one, open the bags and dump out the contents. This mess is what archaeologists call an *assemblage*, or a group of artifacts that are found near each other.

Wearing disposable gloves and being very careful not to cut yourself on any broken glass or sharp edges, sort through the assemblage and find a way to categorize it. You may want to categorize it by material, size, smell, or shape, or come up with your own categories.

Using a permanent marker, label each one-gallon bag with the name for each category. Place the items into it. You may need more than one bag per category.

In your notebook, document the contents of each labeled bag. Describe each item in detail, including its color, size, material, and any food that may still be sticking to it.

STEP THREE: ANALYZING THE ASSEMBLAGE
Now that you have a complete list of your group's trash, it's time to see what that information can tell you about the people who disposed of it.

Pretend you're an archaeologist coming across this pile of trash two hundred years from now. Answer the following questions. Defend your answers using only what the items in the assemblage tell you.

- When did these people live? Is there a written record establishing that date?

- If there's no written record, what time period did they live in? What items helped you establish that time period?

- What did these people eat? Are there items that appear in large numbers? Small numbers? What do these items tell you about their eating habits?

- What activities did these people participate in?

- How many people lived in this group?

- What type of climate did these people live in?

Now look at your two lists of items, the dry list and the wet-and-smelly list.

- What more can you learn about these people with the wet-and-smelly information? Does that information change any of your earlier conclusions?

35

- Does a culture's trash tell you everything you want to know about them? What are the limitations of this sort of research?

- How would the trash of a wealthy culture differ from the trash of a poor culture?

- When trash is collected, it is taken to a dump and mixed together. What would be the challenges of excavating a mixed midden? How would that limit what you could tell about the culture it came from?

FRESH MEAT *profile*

Emily Baker
Steele Accelerated High School
Keller, Texas
Age: 14

You've attended the Texas Archaeological Society's Field School several times. When did you first become interested in archaeology and want to work on a dig?
Since the age of three, I have been in an "ancient Egypt" phase, one that my grandparents thought would be short-lived. Much to their chagrin, it wasn't. I immersed myself in Egyptian culture. I was captivated after reading about what an archaeologist does. I figured the most

prudent way to be the best future archaeologist would be to attend digs while I was still a child, to build a foundation in fieldwork.

Your most recent dig was at the Tait House in Columbus, Texas. What kinds of jobs did you do, and what did the team uncover?
At the Tait House, which was constructed by Charles William Tait around 1857, I helped dig in a pit about twenty feet from the right-hand corner of the house in the Youth Area, which is where kids under fourteen get to dig. We uncovered an assortment of rusted nails, a collection of broken glass, and an abundance of pottery.

How many field schools have you attended? Tell a bit about each school. Where did you dig, what was your job, and what did you uncover at each one?
I have attended three field schools. Each field school lasts ten days. My first and second field schools (2010 and 2011) were in Hondo, Texas. My dad and I uncovered a bunch of skillfully carved projectile points, animal bones, and fire-cracked rock, all of which were painstakingly tedious to excavate. I dug alongside my dad, John, while he was crew chief at a pit during the second field school. My third field school (2013) was at the Tait House, where we uncovered the things I mentioned.

What do you enjoy most about working on archaeological digs?
After excavating in the pits, I enjoy cooling off in the local "watering hole." At the Tait House site, we swam in the Colorado River. Having the ability to cool down in a (somewhat) clean source of running water is a blessing in one-hundred-plus-degree heat.

What is your least favorite part of the work?

Waking up at five o'clock in the morning is my least favorite part of the digs. I've become accustomed to it, but the first morning is definitely a rude awakening.

Where do you see yourself in ten years?

In ten years, I will have just graduated from college, with a bachelor's degree in a scientific field, hopefully physics. Then, I will go to graduate school and obtain an internship or become an assistant to a professional physicist. My lifelong goal is that I will be nothing short of marvelous and a lifelong learner.

The Archaeological Record: Collecting, Reporting, and Analyzing Information

The end of an archaeological dig is not the end of the work; it's the beginning. All the information gleaned from the days and weeks on site is compiled and carefully organized so others can easily access the data and know exactly what work was done. This helps assure that precious and possibly fragile sites are not disturbed more than absolutely necessary.

Archaeologists use computer databases to record and preserve their findings. These databases, along with the physical artifacts, make up what is called the Archaeological Record. One such database is the Digital Archaeological Record (tDAR). It is an international digital warehouse for the storage of digital records of archaeological investigations. The database is maintained by Digital Antiquity, an organization dedicated to promoting the sharing of information and the preservation of the data for future generations.

Besides storing their findings in a database, many archaeologists write articles about their work and publish in journals, magazines, and newsletters. They also present their work at conferences and professional meetings.

3

Learning about the Ancient Dead: Animals and Plants

Paleontologist

Paleontology is the study of the past, mainly through the use of the fossil record. It is a broad field that includes many specific areas of study. Paleontologists use their knowledge of biology, geology, ecology, anthropology, archaeology, and even computer science to understand the process of the life and death of ancient organisms.

Becoming a paleontologist will take the same amount of hard work, study, and field experience as becoming an archaeologist. Plan on getting a bachelor's degree, a master's degree, and probably a doctorate. Don't be discouraged; if you are willing to put in the time and energy, an exciting career awaits you.

Areas of Paleontology

- **Human paleontology or paleoanthropology** is the study of prehistoric human fossils like petrified bones or fossil footprints.

- **Ichnology** is the study of fossil tracks, trails, and footprints.

- **Invertebrate paleontology** is the study of invertebrate fossils. Invertebrates are animals that don't have a backbone, like worms, octopi, and clams.

- **Micropaleontology** is the study of microscopic fossils, including single-celled organisms, pollen, and spores.

- **Paleobotany** is the study of fossil plants, including algae and fungi.

- **Taphonomy** is the study of the process of fossil formation from decay through to their final preservation.

- **Vertebrate paleontology** is the study of vertebrate fossils like primitive fishes and mammals. Vertebrates are animals that have a backbone. Some vertebrate paleontologists are the ones who get to study dinosaurs!

- **Zooarchaeology** is the study of how humans used animals for food or as pets.

ANCIENT HUMAN FOOTPRINTS

In East Africa, west of the Ngorongoro Crater, scientists found 3.6-million-year-old hominid footprints preserved in volcanic rock. There are three separate tracks belonging to a creature who walked upright and stood about four to four and a half feet (1.2 to 1.4 meters) tall.

Although it takes a lot of study to become a paleontologist, there are a lot of people who want to dig for bones but don't want to make it their career. One place where amateurs are always welcome is the Marmarth Research Foundation. Each year they organize fieldwork activities on private land in North Dakota and eastern Montana. The foundation works with scientists to preserve and document the fossil record, but they are dedicated to teaching excited volunteers how to safely and professionally search for dinosaur fossils.

The foundation's founder and current director is Tyler Lyson. He's been finding fossils in the area since he was little. In 1999, when he was a sophomore in high school, he discovered Dakota, the "dinomummy." Dakota was a hadrosaur, a duck-billed dinosaur. But unlike other hadrosaur fossils, this one had scales that were still intact. Excavation began in 2004, and it soon became apparent that there was a whole dinosaur there, skin and all!

The discovery of Dakota was scientifically significant because the body was almost completely intact and the skin was fossilized, which is one of the rarest fossil finds in the world! Because the skin envelope of Dakota did not collapse, he may help unlock many secrets of what went on inside the bodies of dinosaurs.

A team from the National Geographic Society filmed the excavation and made a television documentary called *Dino Autopsy*, which aired in 2007. Parts of Dakota are on display at the North Dakota Heritage Center, and the rest of him is in a nearby lab where sixty-seven million years of rock will need to be removed to reveal what's hidden beneath the skin envelope.

TYLER RANSE LYSON, CURATOR OF VERTEBRATE PALEONTOLOGY, DENVER MUSEUM OF NATURE AND SCIENCE DENVER, COLORADO

When did you first become interested in paleontology and decide to make it the focus of your career?

Some of my earliest childhood memories are of finding fossils. My passion for fossils continued throughout my middle- and high-school years, as I worked for various visiting professors and scientists doing fieldwork near my hometown over the summer months. It was then that my interest in fossils shifted from viewing them as treasure to viewing them as keys to unlocking the answers to many interesting questions surrounding extinct animals.

What education/work path did you take to get where you are today?

I was fortunate to grow up in a very rural area that just happened to be one of the best places in the world to find fossils. As a result, each year, scientists from around the world would flock to my hometown to do their fieldwork. I was able to join them in the field and was exposed to the nuts and bolts of paleontology at a very early age. I attended a small liberal arts school, Swarthmore College, where I majored in biology. My work there helped me sharpen my scientific skills. I then attended Yale University, where I got my PhD in geology and geophysics, and completed my postdoctoral work at the Smithsonian Institution.

Why is a paleontologist's work important?

The fossil record is our only direct window into time and therefore provides valuable data on past life and climate, and changing ecosystems. If we want to have a better understanding of our current world and how it came to be, it's important to have a better understanding of Earth's rich paleontological history. Furthermore, paleontological data is important for helping plan for the future. The earth is constantly changing, and paleontological data provides direct evidence that shows how life responds to these changes.

Why did you choose to focus your research on prehistoric turtles?

Turtles are one of the last major groups of living animals that we don't know where they fit in the tree of life. This is partly because of their bizarre body plan. How do turtles breathe? They are the only animals that lock their ribs up into a shell. But as a result of this, they can no longer use their ribs to breathe, like most other animals. Instead they've developed a unique abdominal muscle-based mechanism, and I'm interested in how and when this evolved.

I'm also interested in how turtles respond to major extinction events, including the meteorite impact 66.06 million years ago that wiped out the dinosaurs. Interestingly, I've found that turtles have done exceptionally well across all of the major extinction events, which speaks to the success of their body plan. Sadly, turtles are currently not doing so well with approximately 49 percent of turtles on the list of threatened animals. Turtles are well adapted for dealing with natural disasters, but are no match against humans who enjoy eating turtle meat and love having turtles as pets.

What is "the chicken from hell"?

Anzu wyliei (aka the chicken from hell) is a dinosaur I helped describe in 2014. I found a partial skeleton of this animal approximately ten years ago. The animal was a large, toothless, feathered omnivore that roamed the floodplains of North and South Dakota and Montana. *Anzu* lived with *Triceratops*, *Edmontosaurus*, and *T. rex*, and was one of the last dinosaurs to dominate the planet.

Tell us what you've learned about dinosaurs and why they went extinct.

Dinosaurs dominated the planet for over 150 million years. I've mostly worked on the dinosaurs that lived right before they went extinct. I've described new species of dinosaur as well as analyzed how the dinosaurs were distributed across the paleo-landscape. The work that I've done, as well as numerous scientists before me, has indicated that dinosaurs went extinct when a large meteorite struck Earth off the Yucatan peninsula in the Gulf Coast 66.06 million years ago. The initial warming and then extended period of darkness and cooling killed the plants and many animals that relied on plants for food, including the dinosaurs.

What advice would you give a young person who is interested in becoming a paleontologist?

Get outside! Start making observations and asking questions about the natural world. Observations and questions are both crucial to being a successful scientist. Pay attention in school, particularly in your science classes, all of them. Both scientific and creative writing is very important. It's important to be able to communicate your results to other scientists as well as the general public. I would also recommend volunteering at your local museum.

What do you see as future trends in paleontology?

I think that by studying the past, we can help plan for the future. There are a number of global crises, including global climate change and an explosion in the number of humans on the planet, as well as a number of associated problems. Thus, I think it is extremely important to study those time periods right before and after major extinction events to get a better understanding of the cause(s) of the extinctions and then the timing of the post-extinction recovery. A better understanding of these extinction events can help us plan for the future.

THOUSANDS OF DINOS!

Seven-year-old Ruth Mason found thousands of dinosaur fossils on her family's ranch in South Dakota. The spot, later named the Ruth Mason Quarry, yielded tens of thousands of dinosaur fossils. Today, many amateur archaeologists flock to this area to uncover ancient bones, and the Children's Museum of Indianapolis sponsors an annual "Dinosaur Dig" at the quarry for families and teachers.

SPOTLIGHT

Roy Chapman Andrews (1884-1960): American Archaeologist, Explorer, and a Real-Life Indiana Jones

Like the fictional character Indiana Jones, Roy Chapman Andrews is known for his many adventures as an archaeologist and explorer. He narrowly escaped death ten times in his first fifteen years of fieldwork. He escaped drowning in two typhoons. He was threatened by a wounded whale, wild dogs, bandits, and Tibetan priests. He survived falling over cliffs and was nearly caught and squished by a giant python.

Andrews was born in Beloit, Wisconsin, on January 26, 1884. He graduated from college in 1906 with a major in English, but he also took classes in archaeology and evolution, which were unusual subjects at that time.

After college, he worked for the American Museum of Natural History in New York City as janitor in the taxidermy department. While he worked at the museum, he finished a master of arts degree in mammalogy, the study of mammals, at Columbia University.

In the 1920s, he led several expeditions into China, including one in 1923, when he was the first person to find dinosaur eggs. Douglas Preston, in his book *Dinosaurs in the Attic: An Excursion into the American Museum of Natural History*, wrote, "Lying on top of the eggs was the fragmentary skeleton of a tiny, toothless dinosaur, which Andrews theorized had been feasting on the eggs when both beast and nest were covered by sand. The eggs were remarkably well preserved . . . The expedition dug up dinosaur eggs from a number of species by the gross, some of which contained delicate, fossilized dinosaur embryos."[1] That same year, Andrews was featured on the cover of the October 29 issue of *Time* magazine.

From 1934 to 1942, he was director of the American Museum of Natural History. Throughout his career, he wrote many books, including the popular children's books *In the Days of the Dinosaurs*, *All About Dinosaurs*, and *All About Whales*. These books are credited with introducing a new generation of scientists to the exciting world of archaeology.

Andrews spent his retirement years writing and speaking about his life as an archaeologist, He died in California in 1960, at the age of seventy-six.

Paleoethnobotanist

Paleoethnobotany, or *archaeobotany*, is the study of ancient plant remains. Scientists study the remains in order to understand how ancient societies lived and interacted with their environment. Scientists in this field of study work on archaeological digs, but their interest is in the plants that are found, not the animals. They are focused on using special techniques to recover and preserve fragile plant remains from around the world.

There are two types of plant fossils. Macrofossils are pieces large enough to be seen and picked up by hand. Microfossils are tiny pieces, seeds, and pollen, which are recovered using flotation. Flotation is when dry soil is put on a screen and water is flushed through it. The lighter material floats off and the heavier material is left on the screen. Once the materials are separated, they are collected, recorded, bagged, and sent to the laboratory for examination under a microscope.

Paleoethnobotanists are often called in to help archaeologists increase their understanding of an ancient people. What did they eat? Were they hunters or farmers? How did they make their clothing? What plants did they use for medicine? Paleoethnobotanists can also help archaeologists discover what the climate was like and how people built their homes many years ago.

Special Tools Used by Paleoethnobotanists

- High-quality, low-magnification binocular microscopes

- High-power microscopes

- Video and digital cameras with attachments for computerized image analysis

- A muffle furnace for experimental charring and ashing

- Electronic scales

- A Soil Moisture Active Passive (SMAP) flotation machine

- Scanning electron microscopes

Paleofeces and Coprolite

Paleoethnobotanists study paleofeces, which is prehistoric dried poop from humans, and coprolite, which is the fossilized poop from animals. Paleofeces can contain DNA, which is the molecule that holds the genetic code for all living things. Unlike bones, which can give scientists the DNA of the human they came from, paleofeces can give them that DNA as well as the DNA from everything the human ate. This information has revealed that ancient humans ate a rich and varied diet which included lots of different plants and animals.

Ancient poop DNA is recovered through a process called the Maillard reaction. As the poop dries out, the sugars from the digested plants or animals react with amino acids and form larger sugar compounds. These large sugar compounds surround and encase the DNA, preserving it for scientists to find thousands of years later.

Hendrik Poinar and Svante Pääbo, from the Max Planck Institute in Munich, Germany, were the first to find DNA in ancient poop. In

1998, they extracted DNA from twenty-thousand-year-old ground sloth poop. They later successfully extracted DNA from the poop of another species of extinct ground sloth and an extinct goat.

DOES ANCIENT POOP STINK?

According to archaeologist Kristin Sobolik, in an article for *Odyssey: Adventures in Science* magazine, the answer is yes! She uses trisodium phosphate to break apart the dried poop and reveal what's inside. This process also releases the smell of the thousand-year-old human waste. "It kind of brings back the life of the stuff," she said.

BRINGING BACK THE WOOLLY MAMMOTH

Scientists in Russia have found blood in a forty-three-thousand-year-old woolly mammoth that was discovered on the Russian island of Maly Lyakhovsky in May 2013. From that blood, they hope to extract DNA that is of high enough quality to allow them to clone the animal.

Although cloning a woolly mammoth is still years away, it is quickly becoming possible. Now is the time for scientists to ask the important question: Should we clone extinct animals? And if we do, how do we responsibly provide protection and habitat for them?

How Old Is It?
Ever wonder how archaeologists figure out how old an artifact is? Most of the processes are complex. They can take a long time and a lot of money to complete. There are archaeologists who specialize in dating artifacts. If figuring out the age of ancient dead things is interesting to you, here are a few ways scientists do it.

Relative Dating

Relative dating is used to determine if one site is older or younger than another. Scientists use *stratigraphy*, the study of layers of rocks and the objects embedded in them, to determine the age of an artifact. This method assumes, and this is usually true, that deeper layers of rock are older than more shallow layers, and that each layer represents an interval of time. Since certain plants and animals lived during specific time periods, their fossils or remains, when found in a layer of rock, help determine the age of the layer. Before the arrival of absolute dating methods in the twentieth century, nearly all dating was relative.

Absolute Dating, or Chronometric Dating

Absolute dating is the more difficult task of determining the year in which human or animal remains were alive or when a geological layer was deposited. Scientists use documents or objects of known age to confirm these dates. They can use historical writings, coins, pottery from established time periods, hieroglyphs, dendrochronology, and radiocarbon dating.

THE GEOLOGICAL TIMESCALE

The geological timescale of the earth is divided into eons, eras, periods, and epochs, with an epoch being a relatively short amount of time in comparison to an eon. Each eon contains several eras, each era contains several periods, and, for the most part, each period contains several epochs, which can represent millions of years.

Each division of time is not defined by specific dates but by characteristics associated with it. Here are five interesting time periods when most of the good stuff happened.

- **Silurian,** 443.4 to 419.2 million years ago (mya). Huge reef systems appear. Fish begin to diversify. Insects and plants begin to appear on land.

- **Carboniferous,** 358.9 to 298.9 mya. Earliest reptiles appear, and vast forests are submerged and later became the coal we burn today.

- **Permian,** 298.9 to 252.17 mya. Only one supercontinent, called Pangea. Period ends with the biggest mass extinction in Earth's history and leads to the age of the dinosaurs.

- **Jurassic,** 201.3 to 145.5 mya. The first birds appear. Big dinosaurs dominate the lush landscape.

- **Quaternary,** 2.58 mya to present. The "Age of Humans," characterized by ice ages and by animals adapting to climate change.

FRESH MEAT
profile

RILEY THE PALEONTOLOGIST
LINCOLN ELEMENTARY SCHOOL
LINCOLN, ALABAMA
AGE: 10

When did you first discover a love for these ancient, extinct animals?
I discovered my love of dinosaurs when I was four years old.

You have a website, rileytalk.com. When and why did you start that site?

I started my website in the summer of 2011 to have all my videos and pictures in one spot. I was getting a lot of views from YouTube and wanted my fans to have a place to see all my fun activities.

You go into classrooms and talk to students about dinosaurs. Why do you go, and what do you teach them?

I love to go to other classrooms to share my love of dinosaurs and teach other kids what I have learned. I teach about what a paleontologist does and tell some interesting facts that they might otherwise never hear. I take the fossils that I have found, and sometimes my pet bearded dragon to show them a modern-day reptile.

What dinosaur fascinates you the most and why? And how do you choose one to be featured on your website?

My favorite dinosaur is *Velociraptor*. It has really cool claws and is very fast. I try to choose a dinosaur for my website that is odd and not very well known. I want people to learn of the ones that don't get much attention.

How do you balance your school visits and website work with your schoolwork and other activities?

It is sometimes hard because I also take piano and guitar lessons. I try to make time for my website and videos on weekends, when I am not on a fossil dig. I have not had much time for videos lately, but I will be making one soon.

Where do you see yourself in ten years?

I plan to be in college studying zoology and biology. These are typical majors to be a paleontologist. I am not sure what college I want to attend at this time.

What is the most exciting paleontology-related thing to happen to you?

The most exciting event was on my first dinosaur dig. We found a *Tylosaur* and I was able to help collect it.

Dendrochronology

Dendrochronology is the study of the annual growth rings in trees. Every year during the growing season, a tree adds a layer of wood cells, consisting of thin-walled cells in the spring and thicker-walled cells in the summer and early fall. These thin- and thick-walled cells make visible circles around the tree.

The wider the ring, the better the conditions were for growth. By studying these rings, scientists called *dendrochronologists* can learn a lot about the environment during the years of a tree's life. For example, they can tell when there was a drought and the tree grew slowly. They can also see damage from fire and when insects invaded an area.

Through the use of dendrochronology and other dating techniques, scientists have verified the origins of paintings and set exact dates for the reigns of ancient kings and for catastrophic natural events. They studied tree rings and dated the Santorini volcanic eruption, one of the largest eruptions in the past ten thousand years, to the late seventeenth century BCE, one hundred years earlier than was originally thought.

Radioactive Decay

Radioactive decay happens when the atoms of a radioactive element disintegrate over time. This disintegration happens naturally and is predictable. Every element decays at its own rate, unaffected by external physical conditions. By measuring the amount of original and transformed atoms in an artifact, scientists can determine the age of that object.

THE LOST COLONY OF ROANOKE

In 1587, a group of colonists sailed from England. They landed on an island off the coast of what is now North Carolina, and became the first Europeans to settle in the New World.

Later that year, their governor, John White, left the settlement and returned to England for supplies. When he returned three years later, the island was deserted, and no trace of the colonists was ever found, except "Cro" carved into a tree and "Croatan" carved in a fence post.

Where the colonists went and what happened to them is still a mystery. However, researcher Dennis Blanton from the College of William and Mary and climatologist David Stahle of the tree ring laboratory at the University of Arkansas may have found a clue. By studying the rings from very old bald cypress, they discovered that from 1587 to 1589, the area had the worst drought of the past eight hundred years. Talk about bad timing for those colonists!

Carbon-14 Dating

To determine the age of ancient organisms, some scientists measure the amount of carbon-14 in a sample, usually charcoal, wood, bone, or shell. Carbon-14 is a radioactive form of carbon. Along with carbon-12, it is created in the atmosphere by cosmic rays. Cosmic rays are invisible, high-energy particles that bombard the earth from space.

When carbon-12 and carbon-14 fall to earth, they are absorbed by plants. The plants are eaten by animals who in turn are eaten by larger animals. Over time, every organism, including humans, absorbs a fixed amount of carbon-12 and carbon-14. The level of carbon molecules is determined by the amount found in the atmosphere. As long as the organism is living, these levels are replenished. When the organism dies, absorption stops.

After death, the carbon-14 in the organism begins to decay and becomes nitrogen-14. The time it takes for half of the carbon-14 to decay is 5,730 years. This is called a half-life. By measuring the amount of carbon-14 that's left and the amount of carbon-12 (which does not decay), scientists can determine the exact date of death.

Conventional radiocarbon dating can measure death dates back forty thousand to fifty thousand years (give or take two thousand years), and sensitive instruments can date back to around seventy thousand years. An accelerator mass spectrometer (AMS) can count carbon-14 atoms and date a sample as small as a single kernel of grain or a fleck of wood. Radiocarbon dates combined with tree ring analysis can pinpoint date of death to within a hundred years.

Since the amount of carbon-14 in the atmosphere has changed over time, scientists must verify how much carbon-14 was in the atmosphere at the time of death in order to calculate absorption and decay rates. This is done using tree-ring analysis, ice-core samples, and coral reef testing.

OTHER DATING METHODS THAT USE THE TRANSFORMATION OF ONE ELEMENT INTO ANOTHER

- **Potassium-argon dating** is used to date volcanic rocks that are between four billion and one hundred thousand years old. Potassium-40 decays to argon-40 with a half-life of 1.26 billion years.

- **Uranium-thorium dating** measures the ratio of uranium-234 to thorium-230. Uranium-234 decays to thorium-230 with a half-life of about 250,000 years.

- **Argon-argon dating** came into favor after scientists realized some limitations in potassium–argon dating. In argon–argon dating, neutrons are used to irradiate a rock sample, which converts the potassium-40 isotope into argon-39. Scientists can then measure the amount of argon-39 in the sample to determine its date.

- **Rubidium-strontium dating** measures the ratio of rubidium-87 isotopes to the stable strontium-87 isotopes, as well as the ratio of strontium-87 isotopes to strontium-86 isotopes. By plotting a graph of these ratios, scientists can determine the exact age of a rock. Rubidium-87 decays to strontium-87 with a half-life of 48.8 billion years.

SPOTLIGHT

Willard Libby, Radiocarbon Dating, and the Nobel Prize

Willard Libby was born in Colorado on December 17, 1908. In 1933, he earned a PhD from the University of California at Berkeley, where he stayed and became an associate professor of chemistry.

When World War II broke out, Libby went to Columbia University to work on the Manhattan District Project, a research project that led to the production of the atomic bombs that were dropped on Hiroshima and Nagasaki, Japan, in 1945.

After the war, Libby worked at the University of Chicago as a professor of chemistry until 1954, when he was appointed by President Dwight D. Eisenhower to the US Atomic Energy Commission. While at the University of Chicago, Libby led a team that developed carbon-14 dating, and in 1960, he was awarded the Nobel Prize in Chemistry for that work.

Libby's book, *Radiocarbon Dating*, was published by the University of Chicago Press in 1952, and he also authored a number of articles in scientific journals. He died in Los Angeles, California, in 1980. He was seventy-one years old.

Electron Spin Resonance

Electron spin resonance (ESR) is a fairly new dating method. It measures electrons captured in bone or shell samples and can date them up to two million years old. Background radiation causes electrons to dislodge from their normal position in atoms and become trapped in the crystalline mesh of the sample. When odd numbers of electrons are separated, there is a measurable change in the magnetic field (or spin) of the atoms. Since the magnetic field changes in a predictable way as a result of this process, it provides an atomic clock that can be used for dating purposes. ESR is used to date calcium carbonate in limestone, flint, coral, fossil teeth, and egg shells.

Thermoluminescent Dating

Thermoluminescence measures energy released from previously heated materials like pottery or rock. When a material is first heated to high temperatures, trapped energy that was stored in certain crystals, like quartz and feldspar, is released. Over time, the rock or pottery is exposed to sunlight or cosmic rays from space and energy is reabsorbed.

Scientists take a sample of rock or pottery and reheat it to over 930 degrees Fahrenheit (500 degrees Celsius). As the sample heats up, energy is released and creates light. The intensity of this light is measured to determine how long it's been since the material was last heated and, thus, how old it is—the older the sample, the more intense the light. Using this thermoluminescence technique, pottery pieces as old as one hundred thousand years have been dated.

Note:

1. Douglas Preston, *Dinosaurs in the Attic: An Excursion into the American Museum of Natural History* (New York: St. Martin's Press, 1986), 101.

4

Caring for the Recent Dead

Although there are interesting jobs working with the ancient dead, you may want to consider one of the many career options that involve caring for the recent dead. From caring for the body of a newly deceased person to helping law enforcement find and identify twenty-year-old remains, the jobs that fall within the sphere of working with the recent dead are as diverse as the people who work in them.

Everything alive today will one day die—including you. But in the meantime, someone has to care for the dead and dispose of their remains. When plants die, they usually fall to the ground and rot, returning their minerals to the earth to be used as nutrients for the next generation of plants. The same thing happens with animals and humans if they are buried and allowed to decay in a natural way.

Unfortunately, sometimes dead animals and dead humans carry diseases. This is why it is important to dispose of their remains in a way that limits the possibility of causing harm to the living. In this chapter, you'll learn about some of the jobs that have sprung up over the centuries to handle that problem and other issues surrounding the recently deceased.

Funeral Director, or Mortician

Funeral directors are people who are in the business of taking care of human remains. They do this by embalming and burial, or through cremation. In most cases, funeral directors are involved in the planning and arrangement of funeral services. They may also dress the deceased, position them in the coffin, and apply makeup or other enhancements to make a dead person presentable for viewing. This is called *cossetting* the deceased.

Traits You Need to Succeed

- A desire to serve others

- A belief in the importance of ceremony for the expression of grief and the acceptance of death

- Tolerance for other peoples' beliefs, faiths, and cultures

- Tolerance for how individuals express grief

- Interest in the science behind preparing a body for burial

- Compassion

- Interest in owning and managing your own business

Funeral Director Responsibilities

- Support the grieving family members during the first days after the loss of their loved one.

- Work with the family to create an appropriate funeral service.

- Arrange transport for the body from the place of death to either the funeral home or the crematorium.

- Prepare the body for burial, following family wishes and the laws of your state.

- Secure information for, and file, death certificates and other legal documents.

- Help families navigate the process of filing for death benefits.

- Help individuals find counseling or support groups to assist them through their mourning period.

Education Requirements in Most States

- A high school diploma or General Educational Development (GED)

- An associate's degree, or equivalent number of college credits, that focuses on areas like public health, biology, business management, the psychology of grief, communications, funeral services law, and professional ethics

- Pass your state or the national board licensing exam

- An internship or apprenticeship of one to three years

- Continuing education to maintain your license

THE FUNERAL HOME INDUSTRY

In 2014, there were 20,915 funeral homes in the United States, and there is a great demand for well-trained professionals.

Funeral homes owned by families, individuals, or closely held companies make up 86 percent of funeral homes. Only 14 percent are owned by publicly traded corporations.

The average funeral home cares for around 113 bodies a year and has three full-time and four part-time employees. In 1960, the average cost of an adult funeral was $708. Fifty years later, it has risen to $7,045.[1]

WORKING STIFF
profile

LAUREN K. LEROY, FUNERAL DIRECTOR
BUFFALO, NEW YORK

When did you first become interested in becoming a funeral director and decide to make it the focus of your career?

I was about twelve years old or so.

I remember going up to my mom and telling her I wanted to be a funeral director. She didn't think I fully understood what that title meant at the time, so she dismissed it. As I got older and continued to tell her that I wanted to become a funeral director, she began to encourage me. But she always made me understand she wouldn't be disappointed if I were to change my mind. My dad was always supportive. He actually went to school to be a funeral director but didn't complete the course. I like to think that I finished what he started. I went to mortuary school right out of high school and got my first real job in a funeral home when I was twenty.

What education/work path did you take to get where you are today?

I completed my associate's degree in funeral services from the New England Institute of Funeral Service Education at Mount Ida College in Newton, MA. In New York State, you're only required to have an associate's degree to practice. I worked part time at a funeral home in Massachusetts while I was in school and over my summer breaks. After I graduated, I got an apprenticeship with a local funeral home outside of Buffalo.

To become licensed, you need to do a one-year apprenticeship and then take the National Board Exam, which is actually two separate tests, what we call the "arts" test and "sciences" test. Then, I had to pass a New York State Funeral Law Exam. After all of that, I was fully licensed and was considered both a funeral director and an embalmer. If you complete everything on time, it's a three-year process.

Will you be a funeral director for the rest of your working years?

It hasn't always been easy. About a year ago, I battled depression and became really sick. When you're constantly working long hours and are surrounded by death, it can take a toll on you. My mom begged me to quit my job and work anywhere else, because my health was suffering so much. She told me to get a retail job and just take a break. After all, I was only twenty-three and had the rest of my life to figure it out.

What I discovered was that funeral directing isn't just a job; it's who I am. So I made a few changes and gave up certain aspects of the job, like embalming and removals. I learned over the previous years that I'm strongest when working directly with the families. And now, here I am, happy and healthy. I always joke around that funeral directors don't retire; they just die (bad joke, yes, but also true). I love what I do, and I could never see myself doing something outside of funeral services.

What fascinates you most about your work, and why is it important?

I meet such amazing people! Unfortunately, it's during one of the worst times of their lives. I love making arrangements because I get to learn about the deceased and their family. Everyone has a story and I love that I am able to help share it. I think that it's important to honor a life lived, no matter how long or short it was. I get to talk with people and explain this to them as we arrange a memorial service, visitation, funeral, whatever works best for their situation.

You encounter people when they are at their most vulnerable. What skills and/or personality traits do you think are important to succeed at your job?

Although I took classes to prepare me for working with the grieving, being able to interact with them goes beyond what you can learn in a classroom. People are not textbooks. There are no rules for what they will do or say. I honestly believe that I interact so well with people because I do not look threatening and I can listen to them.

You have to learn to hear what people are saying even when they're not saying it. And you need to be able to read body language. If someone comes in and sits down in front of me with their arms crossed, I know that they are guarding themselves. I slowly begin to break down the barrier by talking with them, maybe making a small joke if I feel it's appropriate. I want to help people. I like fixing problems. I believe that all of these traits allow me to succeed in my job.

Every day, you encounter grief in its many forms. How do you keep it from overwhelming you?

Keeping grief from overwhelming me was a process that I had to learn. Certain deaths just affect you, like the death of a child or a sudden, tragic death. I had to learn to separate myself from my work. I had learn that even though I was helping people through a loss, these deaths were not my loss.

It's hard to do this job if you don't have a support system. I also take a lot of time for myself. I read a ton of books and am a huge fan of bubble baths!

You have a blog, littlemissfuneral.com. When and why did you decide to share your thoughts online?
I started *Little Miss Funeral* in March 2012. I was twenty-two at the time. At that age, most of my peers hadn't even graduated from college yet, so I had a ton of people who contacted me about my odd career choice. People wanted to know what I did and why I did it. I don't mind sharing my story, but I found that I was repeating the same things over and over to different people.

One day, I was online and just decided to start blogging. Over time, it became more like therapy for me. I would write about good days and bad days in the funeral industry. I'd write about my thoughts and ideas about my job. It's a log of my journey. If you read it, you can see when I was depressed, because those posts have a very negative tone to them. But you can also see how much I love my job.

What advice would you give a young person who is interested in becoming a funeral director?
Being a funeral director is not an easy job, but it's a rewarding job. There are so many small details that go into this profession, and sometimes it can be overwhelming, but you're helping people during a time when they cannot help themselves. If you have a desire to help others, this is the job for you. I think my biggest suggestion would be to take care of yourself. And don't give up. Never give up on your

dream and never let people discourage you from a path that you want to travel down.

What do you see as future trends in mortuary science and the funeral home industry?

Personalized services are a trend that I can see growing. People are starting to get away from cookie-cutter funerals. There is now no such thing as a "normal" funeral. Everyone has a story to tell, and people want their services to be tailored to the life that they lived. I'd love to see more blogging within the funeral industry. Funeral directors can learn so much from one another, and blogging is a great way to reach out to the community that we serve.

Jobs within the Funeral Home Industry

- **Location managers** work for large corporations that own multiple funeral homes. They are responsible for managing a single funeral home and building relationships within the community. They hire, train, and direct funeral home employees and ensure that the facility and equipment are well maintained. They are responsible for budgeting, marketing, and other business operations. They oversee visitations and funerals at the funeral home, and are expected to meet the needs of the clients as well as their family and friends. A location manager usually has a bachelor's degree, is a licensed funeral director, and has management experience.

- **Funeral attendants** set up and work at viewings, funeral services, and memorial services. They interact with families and are responsible for meeting their needs. Requirements for funeral attendants vary according to the needs of the funeral home.

- **Funeral arrangers** work with families to create a memorable funeral or memorial service. They work on multiple cases at one time. They often have an associate's or bachelor's degree and have passed the appropriate funeral services exams. In some cases, funeral arrangers are also funeral directors.

- **Receptionist/clerks** greet potential clients, answer phones, and file paperwork. They may fill out death certificates, print prayer cards, act as notaries public, and complete a variety of office duties. This position is usually filled by a high school graduate with knowledge of computers and office machines, or someone with some college credits.

- **Grief counselors** help people overcome the loss of a loved one. They often work for funeral homes, but also in hospitals, mental health clinics, senior living facilities, or in private practice. To become a grief counselor, you will need a doctorate in psychology.

- **Mortuary cosmeticians**—there are about 230 full-time mortuary cosmeticians in the United States. Most go to cosmetology school or mortuary school and then get on-the-job training to learn the finer techniques of applying makeup on the deceased.

- **Hearse drivers** deliver each body from the place of death to the funeral home, from the funeral home to the grave site, and anywhere else the funeral home or family may direct them to take it. Drivers must have a commercial driver's license.

- **Sales professionals**—as the industry moves forward and more people are preplanning their funerals, there is a need for sales staff. This may involve creating sales presentations, networking within the community, following up on referrals, and presenting informational seminars. A funeral home or cemetery salesperson is hardworking but compassionate. Excelling in this position does not require a college degree, but a clear understanding of customer relations is a plus.

VAULTS, COFFINS, CASKETS, URNS, AND MARKERS

Whenever a body is buried in the ground, it must be housed in a container and the spot identified. There are jobs related to the manufacturing of each of these products.

- **A burial vault** that houses the casket or urn and protects it from the weight of the earth and heavy maintenance equipment that might pass over the grave. It preserves the beauty of the cemetery or memorial park by preventing the ground from settling.

- A container to hold the body. This can be **a coffin**, which is a wooden box with six or eight sides, shaped to resemble a human being, or **a casket**, which is a rigid, rectangular container made from wood or metal and is decorated and lined with fabric.

- A container to hold the cremated remains is called **an urn**. They are usually made from metal and come in many shapes and sizes. There are also biodegradable urns that break down over time.

- **A marker** to show where the body was buried. These can range from a simple, flat-to-the-ground piece of granite with names and dates on it to a large, stand-up granite monument. Today, the smaller flat markers are preferred because a mower can easily drive over them, thus reducing cemetery maintenance costs.

EMMA CRAWFORD COFFIN RACE

Emma Crawford moved to Manitou Springs, Colorado, in 1889. She had tuberculosis and hoped the town's mineral springs and the mountain air would cure her. Unfortunately, two years later, she died. Twelve men, including her fiancé, William Hildebrand, carried her body up 7,200 feet (2,194.5 meters) and buried her at the top of nearby Red Mountain.

In 1929, following years of stormy weather, Emma's coffin broke free and slid down the mountain. Her nameplate, coffin hardware, and a few of her bones were found in the canyon below. Two years later, she was reburied in an unmarked grave.

Each year, beginning in 1995, the residents of Manitou Springs, Colorado, remember this beloved resident by hosting a coffin race down the main street of their town. The event draws about fifteen thousand visitors each year, who watch coffins of various shapes and sizes roll down the road with ghouls, zombies, and other costumed residents running alongside them.

Death Midwife and Funeral Guide

To help families cope with the process of caring for a recently deceased loved one, trained death midwives and funeral guides are entering the funeral scene. They are not doctors, nurses, or funeral directors. They do not have medical training. They are kindhearted individuals who help people die with dignity, and help families embrace the dying process and see death as a natural part of a life's journey.

To train as a death midwife or a funeral guide, there are courses and certification classes available around the country. Knowledge of different faiths and cultures is important, as well as an understanding and tolerance for varying viewpoints about dying, death, and the afterlife.

WATCHING OVER THE DEAD

The Irish believe a dead body should not be left alone from the time of death to the time of burial. Family members stay with the body at night and are relieved during the daytime by friends and neighbors. This is called a *wake*, and it can last up to nine days. Although wakes still occur in parts of Ireland, they are being replaced with simpler and shorter viewings.

In the Jewish culture, bodies are not left unattended after death either. One or several people act as *shomers*, or guardians, when someone dies, staying with the body until it can be buried.

The air force's Air Mobility Command is responsible for accompanying our military dead from battlefields around the world to Dover Air Force Base in Delaware and then home to their families. Every step of the way, the fallen hero, in a flag-draped casket, is carefully watched over and cared for.

FRESH MEAT
profile

HAILEY D. MATTHEWS, FUNERAL DIRECTOR
DENVER, COLORADO
AGE: 24

When did you first become interested in mortuary science and decide to make it the focus of your career?
When I was nineteen, my mom suggested I look into a mortuary science program through a school she had previously taught at. I read about the program and the class requirements and became intrigued. I had never thought of working

in funeral services before. I read more about it online and also spoke with a gentleman who had been a funeral director for twenty-five years; some of that time, he worked as a deputy coroner. I quickly realized that it wasn't the most convenient occupation or the most well paid, but it was very unique and rewarding. This was what I wanted. When I was twenty, I moved to Denver to go to school and pursue my career.

What education/work path did you take to get where you are today?

I began as a certified nursing assistant (CNA), a job that helped me immensely in funeral service. For six years, I physically took care of patients and communicated with their family members. Not only was that job experience relevant, but it also helped me get accepted into mortuary school and land the job that I have now.

I attended Arapahoe Community College and began the general education credits required to apply to the mortuary science program. After two years of going to school full time, I was accepted into the program. I took the fast-track mortuary science core classes for one year, full time, and seventeen credits a semester.

During that year, I was required to embalm a minimum of ten bodies. The embalming was done at a care center of a funeral home, not on campus. Along with embalming, I took classes like Restorative Art, Business Skills, Merchandising, Microbiology, and Bereavement in Society. After my class-work was completed, I had to do a 180-hour internship at a funeral home. I was required to sit in on ten funeral arrangements and help conduct ten services, all in one summer. After that, I took my national board exams for the International Conference of Funeral Service Examining Boards. I was tested in both an arts section and a science section. I am now nationally certified and have my associate's degree of applied science in mortuary science.

What are the duties and responsibilities of your job?

I meet with families for the cremation arrangements of the family members who have passed away. We discuss their lives, what they loved, what they disliked, what they collected, and what their final wishes were. I present them with a price list; we discuss our different cremation packages and the cost that goes with them.

From there, I ask a series of questions to make sure my families know their options. Questions like: do any family members want to do a viewing before the cremation, witness the start of the cremation, take their loved one's fingerprints, or take a lock of the deceased's hair?

Depending on what is going to be done with the cremated remains, I try to help them pick an urn that fits their plan and that also memorializes their loved one.

We go over the vital statistical information of the deceased's life, basic information. This is used to generate the death certificate, which is sent to the doctor or coroner to sign with the cause of death. Once the death certificate is filed with the county the person died in, we can get a burial/cremation permit. Permission to embalm is given verbally or in writing from the family. For cremation, I also go over a cremation authorization that is signed by the legal next of kin.

If the family wishes to have a viewing, visitation, witnessing of the cremation, burial, funeral service, or anything else, I set it up. I schedule everything and remain with the family throughout. I conduct services or arrange for a clergy member to do it. I play the music and arrange the flowers on an altar or around the casket.

Throughout my time with the deceased and his or her family and friends, I make sure that I pay attention to every detail, and I follow up with them on a regular basis. This is an experience people don't go through every day, and they need guidance each step of the way. I try to get everything done in a timely manner while following the family's and deceased's wishes.

What fascinates you most about your work, and why is it important?

How people react and deal with death. People grieve in many different ways and at different times. It is important to understand this because we are here to make the process easier. The more we understand about how the reality of death is dealt with, the more we can help our families with the healing process. Working in funeral service brings me to reality as well. It fascinates me how short life really is, regardless of what age you are when you pass away. There seems to never be enough time. This is important to realize every day—don't take your life or time with people for granted.

What advice would you give a young person who is interested in becoming a funeral director?

I recommend you really do your research. Look into different school programs and see what they offer for classes and how they differ. Go to a reputable funeral home and see if you can sit down and speak with a funeral director for a while. Speaking with a mortuary science instructor would also be beneficial. I honestly don't feel that this is an occupation that a lot of people desire to do. You need to have a caring spirit and patience. You need to be brave and sometimes have a strong stomach.

What do you see as future trends in mortuary science and the funeral industry?

One of the main things that seems to be trending is cremation. Some states have lower cremation rates than others, but they are rising each year. The possibilities of what to do with cremated remains are endless and growing.

I also notice more and more people choosing to personalize the urn or make the service truly unique. More people seem to be having services without much religious connotation.

Another trend on the rise is, of course, green funerals. I think this is something that will become more popular as our population becomes more environmentally conscious.

Death Midwife

Death midwives, also known as *death doulas* or *soul midwives*, support people through the process of dying. They are supportive companions, not medical professionals. They attend to the dying person's needs by addressing fears, being advocates for final wishes, and attending to practical needs. Their main focus is on the person who is dying, whether in the hospital, in a nursing facility, or at home. Their secondary role is as a support to family and friends who come to attend and visit the dying. Their goal is to create a sacred and safe environment, so the process of dying is as dignified and stress-free as possible.

Along with compassionately caring for the needs of the dying, a death midwife may also:

- **Create a sacred space.** This is a table or shelf within view of the dying person. It is filled with photographs, flowers, special foods, or candles. Anything that brings about happy memories and encourages loving conversations.

- **Create a ceremony.** This ceremony is a way of including the dying in the celebration of his or her life. A way to revisit memorable moments and recall precious events. It can be a religious ceremony in a church, a prayer event in a synagogue, or a secular service in a nature setting.

- **Care for the dead.** After a loved one has died, sometimes the family is in shock, and simple decisions can be overwhelming. If needed, death midwives may help with funeral arrangements and filling out paperwork. Their skills may be needed if there is conflict between family members.

- **Help with memorial services.** They may help with planning a funeral service, escort the family to and from the funeral home, and guide them through the process of choosing a gravesite, casket, cards, or headstone. Their focus is on helping the mourning family and friends through the difficult process of burying their dead.

HOME FUNERALS

Over the past century, care for the dying has moved from the bedroom into the hospital room. The preparation of the body for burial has also been taken from the loving hands of family members and placed in the hands of professionals and businesses.

Home funerals are a response to what some feel has become a clinical, soulless experience. Instead of having a service in a church or at a funeral home, some families are opting for a funeral or life celebration at home. This is gaining in popularity, as families return to past traditions that offer a more intimate setting for their final farewell. For home funerals, the body usually remains at home, is not embalmed, and is cared for by family members.

Home Funeral Guide

Home funeral guides help families through the process of caring for and burying their dead. They help plan and arrange home funerals, prepare the body for viewing, transport the body to a funeral home or crematory, help with paperwork, and try to create a peaceful space so family and friends can grieve. They often work alongside a funeral director, caring for the specific needs of the deceased's family.

Crematory Operator

In most countries, cremation happens in a crematorium. The body is placed in a furnace and burned at 1,400 to 1,800 degrees Fahrenheit (760 to 982 degrees Celsius) for two to two and a half hours. At that temperature, all the organic material is consumed and only fragments of bone remain. The cremains (cremated remains) are then placed in a container or urn and given to the family or the funeral home. Cremains are not a health threat, and they can safely be buried or scattered.

Crematory operators remove and transport the body from the place of death. They conduct cremations and maintain proper documentation. They ensure that the cremains are released or delivered to the proper facility or person.

They are responsible for facility maintenance and documentation. A crematory operator must complete training at a college or technical school that specializes in funeral service and mortuary science, and pass the appropriate exams required for certification to cremate human remains. It is important to note that in this position, there is a possibility of exposure to dangerous chemicals or diseases.

The History of Cremation

Most scholars agree that cremation was happening at around 3000 BCE and probably earlier. The practice spread across northern Europe and western Russia, and by 1000 BCE, it was happening in Britain, Spain, and Portugal. By 800 BCE, it was common in ancient Greece and was an important part of their burial custom. However, by 400 CE, earth burial had completely replaced cremation, except for rare instances of plague or war. This preference remained popular for the next 1,500 years.

Modern cremation began when Italian doctor Bruno Brunetti developed a dependable cremation chamber. He displayed his invention at the 1873 Vienna Exposition, but it couldn't be used because cremation was illegal in his country. In 1874, Frederick Siemens built a furnace in Germany and performed the first modern cremation, which started a cremation movement on both sides of the Atlantic.

- 1874: The Cremation Society of England is founded by the Physician to Queen Victoria, Sir Henry Thompson.

- 1876: The first North American cremation chamber is built by Dr. Francis Julius LeMoyne in Washington, Pennsylvania.

- 1885: Jeannette Pickersgill becomes the first person to be legally cremated in England.

- 1900: There are twenty crematories in operation in the United States.

- 1913: The Cremation Association of America is founded by Dr. Hugo Erichsen. This year, there are fifty-two crematories and over ten thousand cremations.

- 1975: The Cremation Association changes its name to the Cremation Association of North America to include crematories in Canada among their members. By this time, there are 425 crematories and nearly 150,000 cremations being done each year.

- 2009: There are 2,100 crematories and over 900,000 cremations, 36.84 percent of all deaths in the United States.

- It is expected that cremation will be used in over 50 percent of all deaths in the United States by 2018, with Nevada, Washington, and Oregon having the highest rates.

- In Japan, the cremation rate is almost 100 percent. That country is closely followed by Taiwan, Hong Kong, and Switzerland, which all have rates over 80 percent.

FRESH MEAT profile

MELANIE NEDDOW, LICENSED FUNERAL DIRECTOR
DETROIT, MICHIGAN
AGE: 22

When did you first become interested in mortuary science and decide to make it the focus of your career?
This was never a family business or something any of my friends were ever interested in. I guess attending funerals at a young age planted the idea in my head. I never thought of it seriously until high school, when a cousin of mine committed suicide. It was at his visitation that I got very curious about the work.

What education/work path did you take to get where you are today?
I was always interested in science and health science classes. I took science courses in high school, including AP biology and health occupations. They helped me a lot once I headed off to college.

My two years of prerequisite coursework for the mortuary science program at Wayne State University included classes in microbiology, anatomy, physiology, chemistry, and psychology. After I finished those, I was accepted into the mortuary science program.

The state of Michigan requires a six-month apprenticeship, and I completed mine with Lynch & Sons Funeral Directors. I took my national and state board examinations and passed them both. Now I am licensed.

Where I am from, we only have one funeral home in about a forty-five-mile radius. I tried to get some hours there, but they never needed the extra help. I worried about going to mortuary school without ever actually working in a funeral home, but I wasn't alone. Most of my class had never worked in a funeral home before, and there were only a handful of students who came from families in the business.

What are the duties and responsibilities of your job?

I greet people and answer phones. I meet with families for pre-need (before the death occurs) and at-need (after the death occurs) arrangements. I transfer decedents from the place of death back to the funeral home. I embalm them, dress them, put cosmetics on them, casket them, or any other preparation work that needs to be done. I make arrangements with the cemetery or crematory, and file all the necessary documents and paperwork. I arrange for clergy to perform services, contact churches, write obituaries and death notices, and submit them to the news-papers. I arrange flowers and clean up the building. I line up cars for the funeral procession. I also do any necessary office work, including making prayer cards, memorial folders, acknowl-edgement cards, etc.

What fascinates you most about your work, and why is it important?

The preparation of the bodies. Whether it's simply cleaning them up and closing their mouths or embalming them and performing restorative work. Seeing the transformation is incredible, and being able to give a family time to say good-bye or a chance to say a proper farewell is so important. I have learned, not only from work and others in this business, but from my own experiences with death, that it is important to be able to see your dead, to touch your dead, to pray, or to cry over your dead, in order to truly say good-bye. Sometimes we have to actually witness something to realize it is real.

What advice would you give a young person who is interested in becoming a funeral director?

Get some experience before entering mortuary school, find part-time work swinging the door at a visitation, placing flowers, or answering the phone. The only way to truly know if you want to do this kind of work is to do the work. There is an ongoing joke here at my funeral home that whenever we encounter a new experience or something strange where we have to improvise, we will look at each other and say, "I didn't learn this in mortuary school!"

Also, being a funeral director is not always easy. You will have long, difficult days; you will miss some holidays and vacations; you will get woken up at four in the morning by a grieving family who needs your help; your hard work will sometimes go unnoticed; you will sometimes feel unappreciated and overworked; but it just takes that one family member to give you a hug and tell you how they couldn't have gotten through this time without you that makes it all worth it.

What do you see as future trends in mortuary science and the funeral industry?

Women entering the field. For years funeral service was a business dominated by men, but today the majority of mortuary science graduates are women. I predict this percentage will continue to grow. Women are so compassionate and caring, have such a great eye for detail, etc. We have so many great qualities that make us perfect for this career.

Note:
1. "NFDA Releases Results of Member General Price List Survey," National Funeral Directors Association, August 1, 2013, http://nfda.org/news-a-events/all-press-releases/3719-nfda-releases -results-of-member-general-price-list-survey.html.

5

preserving the Dead

From ancient Egypt, when bodies were mummified to make a home for the soul, to the twentieth century, when the Soviet Union's premier Vladimir Lenin's body was embalmed for political purposes, humans have tried to preserve dead bodies. Today, most human bodies are preserved through a process called *embalming*. It is mainly done so the body will look good for the funeral, which can sometimes take place a week or more after death.

Preserving Human Bodies

What Is Embalming?

Embalming is the process where fluids are removed from the body and then replaced with chemicals that sanitize and preserve the remains. There are two types of embalming fluids.

Formaldehyde has been used in the United States since the late 1800s and is inexpensive. With mounting health and environmental concerns over the use of formaldehyde, scientists are looking for alternatives.

Glutaraldehyde is one alternative to formaldehyde. It irritates the skin and eyes, but there are no studies linking it to cancer, like there are for formaldehyde. For now, it is considered a "green" alternative.

RELIGIOUS RULES ABOUT EMBALMING

- In the **Muslim faith,** embalming is prohibited unless required by law. The body is considered sacred and is buried within twenty-four hours of death. Usually, the body is wrapped in a plain, white burial shroud and laid to rest in a grave without a coffin.

- Most **Christians** allow embalming. However, there are a few groups that prohibit or discourage it unless it's required by law.

- **Neopagans** discourage embalming. They think it disrupts the natural process of decomposition. They encourage placing the body in a biodegradable coffin and burying it under a tree, instead of placing a tombstone.

- Those of the **Bahá'í faith** do not embalm. They wash the body and wrap it in a shroud made from cotton, linen, or silk. The body is buried within a one-hour journey from the place of death. Cremation is also forbidden.

- Traditional **Jewish law** forbids embalming or cremation since burial is within twenty-four hours of death. There are exceptions, but only with the permission of a rabbi or the local Jewish Burial Society.

Trade Embalmer

While most funeral directors are also licensed embalmers, there are people whose work is only to embalm bodies. Trade embalmers often work for more than one funeral home. Besides embalming bodies, embalmers also do restorative and cosmetic work, dress the deceased, and place them in their caskets.

Embalmers are not part of the funeral process; they work behind the scenes. Their focus is on preserving the body for the funeral and preparing the body for viewing and burial. Depending on demand, trade embalmers can make more money than the average funeral director, but they do not receive any of the benefits of full-time employees.

Embalming is recommended whenever a body will be seen by the public. It sanitizes the remains and helps prevent the spread of diseases. If the body was ravaged by disease, decomposition, or trauma, embalming allows the embalmer to give the body a more pleasing appearance. Embalming is also required when the body is stored without refrigeration or if it must be transported on an airplane.

If a body is not embalmed, it begins to decay immediately. Enzymes and bacteria break down the tissue and cause extreme swelling. The skin quickly breaks down, and the body begins to smell in about forty-eight hours, depending on the climate. Bodies that are not embalmed should be buried within a day or two.

History of Embalming

The earliest descriptions of embalming come from the Egyptians, who mummified their dead to preserve them for the afterlife. It is estimated that from 6000 BCE to 600 CE, the Egyptians mummified approximately four hundred million bodies. But they weren't the only ones. It was also a practice among the ancient people who lived in Ethiopia, Peru, North America, and the Canary Islands.

OTHER PRE-BURIAL RITUALS:

♀ The Babylonians, Persians, and Syrians placed their dead in jars of honey and wax which kept out the air, and thus the body didn't decay.

- Jews covered their dead in oils and spices and wrapped them in linen.

- Greeks placed coins in the mouth of the deceased to pay passage into the afterlife. They placed cakes of honey by the body to appease the three-headed dog, Cerebus, who guarded the entrance into Hades. They practiced cremation starting in about 300 BCE.

- The Romans washed the body every day for seven days using hot water and oil. Slaves called *pollinctores* performed this duty.

Starting in the fifteenth century, interest in preserving bodies increased as scientists demanded more information about human anatomy and the causes of disease. Discoveries in medicine and embalming were furthered by these scientists.

- **Leonardo da Vinci** (1452–1519) studied human anatomy and produced hundreds of pictures of the inside of the human body.

- **Dr. William Harvey** (1578–1657) was an English physician who discovered how blood circulated throughout the body.

- **Antonie van Leeuwenhoek** (1632–1723) made his own microscope and discovered bacteria in 1683.

- **Dr. Frederik Ruysch** (1638–1731) is thought to be the first to use arterial embalming.

♀ **Alexander Butlerov** (1828–1886) and **Wilhelm von Hofmann** (1818–1892) are credited with the discovery of formaldehyde.

By the early 1900s, local carpenters and cabinetmakers were making coffins. Over time, these men began to "undertake," or assume the responsibility for, other services for those burying their dead. They became known as *undertakers*.

Undertakers took one- or two-day classes from the embalming fluid manufacturers and earned certificates as embalmers. However, by the 1930s, embalmers were required to obtain state-issued licenses. As embalming became more popular, the need for a hasty burial was gone. This gave the deceased's family more time to arrange more elaborate funerals.

SPOTLIGHT

Dr. Thomas Holmes: The Father of Embalming

Thomas Holmes was a physician who graduated from Columbia University's College of Physicians and Surgeons in 1845. At the time Thomas was in medical school, it was difficult to find bodies for the students to study. Bodies preserved on ice or in airtight containers didn't last long before decomposition set in. And bodies that were embalmed with the European method of replacing the body's fluids with highly toxic chemicals like mercury made students fall ill or even die.

After medical school, Holmes began researching different solutions to use for embalming bodies. Eventually, he invented his own fluid pump and started using his own arsenic-based solution. He became well-known for his embalming techniques and sold his solution to surgeons, anatomists, and undertakers around the country.

When the Civil War broke out, the need for embalming increased as the number of dead mounted and families requested that their loved ones be sent home for burial. When Colonel Elmer E. Ellsworth was fatally shot in 1861—the first officer to die in the war—Holmes was a captain in the Union Army Medical Corps and offered to embalm the body for free. At Ellsworth's funeral, the body was on display and everyone was impressed by how lifelike the body appeared.

As a result of the Ellsworth embalming, President Abraham Lincoln asked Holmes to train embalming surgeons who could go to the battlefield, embalm Union soldiers, and send them home to their families for burial.

After his assassination in 1865, President Lincoln was embalmed using Holmes's solution. The president's remains traveled across the country, and thousands of people saw how well embalming could preserve a body.

After the war, Holmes retired to Brooklyn and sold root beer and embalming supplies. There were stories that said he had embalmed bodies stored in his closets and heads sitting on his parlor tables. His strange behavior, probably due to arsenic poisoning, landed him in and out of mental institutions until his death in 1900. It's interesting to note that, when he died, he left instructions that his body was not to be embalmed.

CREATING ANCIENT MUMMIES

The ancient Egyptians are best known for preserving their dead as mummies. They practiced it for over two thousand years and got quite good at it. Here's how it was done.

1. They removed all the internal organs, including the brain, leaving only the heart in the chest because they thought it held the essence of the person. The organs were preserved separately in jars called *canopic jars* and buried with the mummy.

2. They treated the body, inside and out, with natron, a type of salt that absorbs large amounts of liquid.

3. Once the body was dry, they wrapped it using hundreds of yards of linen. Between each layer, they put down a coat of resin and, for protection against evil spirits, included amulets and wrote prayers and magical words on the linen strips.

OLDEST MUMMY

The oldest known human-made mummy is the body of a child. He or she was a member of the South American Chinchorro culture, known for their dedication to preserving the dead. The child lived in the Camarones Valley, south of the port city of Arica in Chile. Her mummified remains were radiocarbon dated to around 5050 BCE.

Cryonics

Cryonics is the preservation of a human body at low temperatures, –320 degrees Fahrenheit (–195 degrees Celsius). People have their bodies frozen in the hope that one day, science will find a way to bring them back to life, heal their diseases, and return them to their former youth and vitality. No one has ever been brought back to life after this procedure, but they have spent thousands of dollars to keep hope alive.

People who are frozen are called *cryopreserved patients*, since they are not considered inescapably dead. Since 1967, when Dr. James Bedford became the first person to be frozen with the intention of being revived, to today, over 240 people have been cryopreserved. Alcor Life Extension Foundation and the Cryonics Institute are the only facilities in the United States that offer this service.

Cryonics is a controversial area of study. If it interests you, consider a career in one of the scientific fields that surround it and hope that you can apply your skills to cryonics in the future. In order for cryopreserved humans to have any hope of being thawed out and returned to life, they will have to wait for important scientific discoveries from the research of the following scientists and fields of study.

Cryobiologists—scientists who study how organisms tolerate cold temperatures. They conduct research on ways to reverse the cold preservation of cells and tissues.

Cryogenicists—scientists who study the effects of low temperatures on the body at a cellular and molecular level. The study of cryogenics uses research from physics and engineering to find ways to produce very low temperatures and study how materials behave at those temperatures.

Nanotech scientists—nanotechnology is the science of modifying objects at the atomic or molecular level. At that level, things are measured in nanometers. One nanometer is equal to one-billionth of a meter. A single human hair is about one hundred thousand nanometers wide. A nanotech scientist builds objects molecule by molecule with results that are nearly perfect in terms of performance, effectiveness, and longevity.

Rheologists—scientists who study how matter flows and deforms under certain conditions. Usually they study liquids, but they also study "soft solids," like mud, sludge, silicate, body fluids, and other matter. Rheologists may also study physics, chemistry, biology, engineering, and mathematics.

Cryoelectronics—a branch in the study of electronics. Scientists study, design, and manufacture components that function at low temperatures, especially using superconductivity. Superconductivity happens when certain materials are cooled and there is no longer any electrical resistance or expulsion of magnetic fields.

Cryoethics—the study of the ethical questions surrounding cryonics, questions like: Is it right to defy death? Is one life worth the cost of preserving the person for possibly hundreds of years? Will it ever be possible to revive people, and if not, how long should they stay frozen? What will life be like for people who are revived long after everyone they have known and loved is gone?

RESEARCH AREAS RELEVANT TO CRYONICS

- **Cerebral resuscitation**—the study of better methods of initial treatment of cryonic patients, as well as looking to discover ways to better freeze the brain and then revive it to retain memories and intelligence.

- **Organ cryopreservation**—the study of better methods of long-term preservation of organs and tissue.

- **Neuroscience**—the study of developing ways of validating preservation methods through better understanding of the neuron activity in the brain.

Preserving Animal Bodies

Taxidermist

Taxidermists prepare and mount the skins of animals for display or for study. They can work on all vertebrates, including mammals, fish, birds, reptiles, and amphibians. Besides the wall of someone's home, taxidermists' work is displayed in restaurants, businesses, educational institutions, and museums.

Today, many parts of the animal are re-created using man-made materials. For example, the eyes are made of glass, the eyelids are sculpted using clay, noses and mouths are formed using epoxy or wax, and the form or body of the animal is created from polyurethane foam. In most cases, only the skin and horns or antlers are natural. And when it comes to fish, sometimes they are completely man-made. This is ideal for those who catch and release their fish, but want life-sized trophies to hang on their walls.

FRESH MEAT *profile*

Leah Johnstone, Leah Johnstone's Taxidermy
Queen Elizabeth Sixth Form College
Gainford Village, Teesdale, County Durham,
England
Age: 17

How did you first discover your love for taxidermy?
One day when I was three years old, my mum was sick, and dad brought some work home to do in the garage, so he could look after me while working. To entertain me, he gave me some wood wool and string and showed me a mannequin,

then told me to copy it. I made a basic mannequin—no wires or anything—and being three, it was obviously useless, but in that time Dad taught me to say "I want to be a taxidermist like daddy," and it stuck.

Not only do I like doing taxidermy, but I also like researching all different aspects of it. I am constantly reading and referring to books on the subject. I even think about mounts I want to do in the future and plan them when I'm bored.

What training did you go through to learn to be a taxidermist?

When I was eleven, I did my first piece—a mole. My dad demonstrated and talked me through the whole process. In December 2010, I completed my second piece, a stoat [short-tailed weasel]. A year or so later, I completed the first piece I sold.

Dad skinned a crow, and I watched, making notes. I then skinned and mounted my own crow, only asking for help when I needed it. Since then, I have pretty much skinned and mounted birds independently, referring to my notes the first few times but still receiving invaluable help from dad. He really was the best teacher! I think nowadays interested people take courses to learn taxidermy and try to cram it all into a day or a week, but Dad and I worked at my own pace. When I was learning, it didn't feel like a lesson. It was just fun, and I think that's the way it should be.

You work a lot with birds. What is it about them that fascinates you?

Every feather has to be in exactly the right place, and that provides a challenge. They look majestic when they are finished! I find them interesting and love learning the anatomy of the bird, which you inevitably start to pick up as you do taxidermy.

For generations, my family has been into bird watching, and we love seeing birds and wildlife in their natural habitat. Dad and I always feel it is a great shame when we get birds in. Often they look perfect but are, sadly, dead. I feel in some way, we are honoring them by preserving them. I do some mammals, however, and recently I did a long-tailed field mouse as a commission, and I was happy with how it turned out.

You have a website, leahjohnstonetaxidermy.weebly.com. When and why did you start that site?
I started my website in June 2014 to coincide with my Facebook page. It allows people to see what I have for sale. I enjoy maintaining it; however, I get most of my commissions through my Facebook page.

How do you balance your taxidermy work with school and your other activities?
I am currently at Queen Elizabeth Sixth Form College, studying economics, biology, geography, and world development. Studying takes up a lot of time, especially when I begin preparation for exams. At that time, I barely do any taxidermy. When I am not studying for exams, I do taxidermy on weekends, school holidays, and the odd evening.

Scouting also plays a big role in my life. I am an Explorer Scout at First Staindrop Explorers, and I have completed my Platinum Chief Scout Award, using taxidermy as my skill section. I have been a Young Leader at First Gainford Scouts for almost four years, and I will become a full leader in January, when my training is complete.

Where do you see yourself in ten years?
Graduated from university with an honors degree in international business. I would love to have lived or be living in Germany for a year. I also want to travel a lot; I want to see places all over the world. I think in ten years I will still be doing taxidermy, however not as a full-time job, more as a hobby. I want my house to be filled with taxidermy, but not just my own. I would love to own a Van Ingen tiger head

[world-renowned taxidermists from India, Van Ingen & Van Ingen Taxidermy, 1890s–1999]. I love the eyes and have done quite a bit of research on taxidermy from that era.

What is the most exciting animal you've worked on, or which project makes you the most proud of your work, and why?
My favorite project was the second magpie I did. I was proud of the finished product and knew the time and effort I put in was worth it. Unfortunately, due to selling it so quickly, I only have one photo of it with a white background. I had planned this piece for ages and was happy with how it looked at the time.

Becoming a taxidermist does not require a college degree. You can find four-, six-, or eight-week classes at taxidermy schools, or take classes at a local trade school or community college. After training, you can get licensed by your state. Each state's requirements may vary, but information can usually be found at the Department of Fish and Wildlife. After receiving a state license, you can apply for a federal permit through the US Fish and Wildlife Service if you want to work on migratory birds.

The National Taxidermists Association (NTA) also offers voluntary certifications that can help you stand out in this field. A certificate from the NTA will require that you enter competitions judged by NTA members. There are four certificates available: mammal, fish, birds, and reptiles.

Taxidermy is a career that depends on word-of-mouth recommendations. It would be wise to find a paid or volunteer position as a taxidermist's apprentice. Learning the subtle skills and tricks of the trade at the start of your career will help you establish a great reputation. To become a highly skilled taxidermist, be prepared to learn carpentry, woodworking, tanning, molding, and casting.

And there is an artistic side to the trade. You will need to know how to sculpt, paint, and draw. In addition to those skills, a few courses in business and website design may be helpful, since most taxidermists own their own businesses.

Other Jobs in the Field

- **Taxidermist's apprentice**—someone who is interested in the work and who is either self-taught or has some training through online classes or by attending a trade school or community college.

- **Teacher**—once you are a well-established taxidermist, you may further your career by teaching classes to individuals or groups. This may be done on your own or through an educational institution. Be aware that some educational institutions may require that you have a bachelor's degree or a master's degree in some related subject, like business or communications.

- **Manufacturing and sales**—work in companies that make animal forms, eyes, nosepieces, and other parts and accessories needed by taxidermists. Most of these jobs would not require an education beyond high school.

- **Mount builder**—free-standing animals are sometimes placed on display mounts that give a sense of the animal's natural habitat: a deer in a field of grass, a mountain goat perched on a rock, or a cougar clinging to a tree branch. Other animals are hung on the wall on mounts that are designed specifically for the individuals ordering them. This is a specialized, hands-on job, but for the right person, it could be rewarding.

INTERESTING ANIMALS OF TAXIDERMY

- Roy Rogers, a famous singer and cowboy actor of the 1950s and 1960s, had his favorite horse, Trigger, preserved through the use of taxidermy. The horse's skin was mounted over a plaster mold and displayed to look like he was rearing up on his hind legs. Beside Trigger were the mounted remains of Buttermilk, which was the horse his wife, Dale Evans, rode, along with Bullet, their German shepherd.

- A male African elephant is the largest mammal ever mounted for a museum. It took the museum's taxidermists sixteen months to do the work. The hide alone weighed two tons. When it was finished in 1959, it was displayed in the rotunda of the Smithsonian Institution National Museum of Natural History in Washington, DC.

- The oldest example of taxidermy is a crocodile that resides in the Natural History and Art Museum in St. Gallen, Switzerland. The croc was preserved in 1623 and is now over 350 years old!

- William Temple Hornaday was America's greatest taxidermist in the late 1800s and early 1900s. In 1888, he heard that there were only three hundred bison left in the wild. He decided to kill and preserve twelve of them for future generations to see. Although this seems outrageous now, his work helped save the animal from extinction. With the help of then-future-president Theodore Roosevelt, he founded the American Bison Society. The society captured some of the few remaining bison, bred them, and reintroduced their offspring into the wild.

History of Taxidermy

The first taxidermists were tanners who skinned animals and preserved their pelts for use in clothing, shoes, and furniture. The demand for quality leather and fur grew, and by the 1700s, there was a tanner in every village.

In the 1800s, hunters started asking upholstery shops to sew up their animal skins and stuff them with cotton or rags. This produced a crude and often ugly reproduction of the original animal. Over time, some parts of the animal, like the mouth and nose, would rot and make the animal unsuitable for display.

By the mid-1800s, arsenic was being used as a preservative, and its use increased the quality of the taxidermists' product. Hunters, scientists, and educators demanded more mounted animals for museums, classrooms, and their homes. Arsenic, despite the fact that it is a poison, remained in use in museums around the world until the 1980s.

EROSION CASTING

Erosion casting is a technique in taxidermy that can produce startlingly lifelike results. The process involves coating the corpse of an animal with a product like silicone, letting it dry until hard, and allowing the corpse to rot. When the process is complete, you are left with a perfect impression of the animal, including every wrinkle and scar.

Taxidermy grew in popularity from the early 1900s onward as wealthy people around the world, especially big-game hunters, demanded wild animals for display in their homes. Then, in the 1970s, the stuffing of animals stopped. Taxidermists began to stretch animal skins over sculpted molds and began using clay, polyurethane foam, wax, and epoxy resins to create a more realistic mounted animal. Today, taxidermists never use the word *stuffed* to describe their animals; they prefer the term *mounted*.

Modern taxidermy techniques were used to create educational and scientific specimens. In a time before cameras, explorers from Europe who encountered a new and strange animal would use taxidermy to preserve it for transport back home. These animals were destined for display at museums and universities or for study by scientists. As techniques progressed, animals were mounted in ever more lifelike poses, eventually leading to the production of dioramas of animals in their natural habitats.

BIRD FANS

In Victorian times, women carried around fans made from preserved birds. The common pigeon and other wild birds were stuffed and then positioned with their wings spread wide in the shape of a fan.

Animal Mummies

Some animals have also been mummified. The largest number of mummified cats was found by an Egyptian farmer in 1888. He uncovered hundreds of thousands of cat mummies while digging near the village of Istabl Antar in northern Egypt.

Besides cats, the Egyptians also mummified birds, crocodiles, baboons, fishes, and even some bulls. Why? Probably for four reasons: food in the afterlife, companionship in the afterlife, an offering to a god, or as a symbol of a god that could be worshipped in the afterlife.

Mummified dogs were found in a thousand-year-old human cemetery in Peru. Anthropologist Sonia Guillen and her team uncovered more than forty mummified dogs. They were buried with their humans, who lived in the Chiribaya culture that prospered from 900 CE to 1350 CE.

WORKING STIFF *profile*

RODNEY SCHOTT, OWNER OF SCHOTT TAXIDERMY, LLC
HELOTES, TEXAS

When did you first become interested in becoming a taxidermist and decide to make it the focus of your career?
At the age of nine, when I had a deer that I harvested taken to a taxidermist to be mounted.

What education/work path did you take to get where you are today, including what you did as a teenager?
Taxidermy is an art, and although the basics can be learned by looking online or going to schools that offer short courses, to really learn the art, you need to work or apprentice under somebody. This was what I did, starting at the age of sixteen and continuing until I opened my own studio at twenty-one.

Would you explain what a taxidermist does and why it's important?
A taxidermist preserves the animal for future generations to enjoy, but more importantly for the hunter to relive the hunt.

Taxidermists are also small business owners. Can you explain the pros and cons of owning a taxidermy business?
As a small business owner, I'm faced with all the problems other business owners have—the burden of being overtaxed

just because of being a business entity; property taxes; permits, which are another form of taxes; and the sales tax that a business is responsible for collecting for the state. Another issue is the liability of owning a business and the problem of finding enough qualified employees.

You go on hunting trips in other countries. Where do you go, why do you go, and what do you bring back?
I've been on hunting trips to Canada: British Columbia, Northwest Territories, Yukon, Alberta; in the United States: Kansas, Montana, Wyoming, Colorado; and in Mexico, New Zealand, and Africa.

I go on these trips for two reasons. I am a hunter myself, so I have an interest in hunting the different species that are indigenous to each area. The second reason is work related. I usually accompany my clients to ensure that the animals taken on the hunt receive proper care, so they can be properly preserved later in my studio.

What was the most interesting/difficult animal you've worked with and why?
I think that the large reptiles are the most difficult to work with, alligators and crocodiles. They are challenging because their skin is unforgiving. It doesn't stretch, and it is hard to sew.

What skills and/or personality traits do you think are important to succeed in your profession?
In this career, as with many others, the hardest part is dealing with the public. You need good people skills to run any business, but as a taxidermist, you also need artistic skills to succeed.

What advice would you give a young person who is interested in becoming a taxidermist?

That it's a rewarding career. That it has its challenges, especially because it's really hard to get your foot in the door. But don't let that deter you. Persevere.

What do you see as future trends in taxidermy?

I see the future of taxidermy as being somewhat in jeopardy. The anti-hunting people are growing in numbers and the media is against hunting as a whole. The more generations who grow up without knowing about hunting as a way of life, the harder it will be to become a successful taxidermist. That said, the taxidermists who succeed will be the ones who produce a very high quality of work.

Nature's Way of Preserving Ancient Plants and Animals

The Fossil Record

A fossil is the preserved remains, usually in stone, of a plant or animal that is over ten thousand years old. There are two types: body fossils and trace fossils. Body fossils are the remains of a plant or an animal's body. Trace fossils are the remains of other things, like footprints or fossilized eggs and nests.

Preservation of remains can happen in several ways. They can be buried in ice or permafrost like the woolly mammoths of Siberia, dried like the mummies of Egypt, or encased in tree resin like insects found in amber. However, the most common way is through petrification, the process of turning organic matter into stone.

REALLY OLD PRESERVED REMAINS

- ○ The oldest frozen human remains were discovered in northern Italy. The man, along with his clothes and tools, died about 5,300 years ago. Even his tattoos were preserved by the extreme cold.

- ○ The oldest animal life found in amber are 220-million-year-old single-celled organisms.

- ○ Frozen wooly mammoths found in Siberia are over 35,000 years old.

- ○ The oldest naturally mummified remains are those of a severed head. It is about six thousand years old and was found in South America.

   Petrification occurs through the process of permineralization. Permineralization happens when a plant or animal is quickly buried, by a mudslide or by sinking into a bog. Ground water, which contains minerals, fills up all the empty spaces in and around it, including its pores and cells.

   Slowly, the water disappears, leaving only minerals behind. It's a complicated process, but basically, even cell walls and membranes can be preserved by trading their carbon molecules for rock-forming minerals. When the process is complete, what was once bone is now rock in the shape of a bone, or rock in the shape of a plant.

   If you want to look for fossils but don't want to go to school to become a professional, some organizations will guide you and allow you to work with them. No matter where you look for fossils, it is important that you follow the rules of fossil collecting, so you don't accidently destroy important artifacts.

ONE-HUNDRED-TWENTY-FIVE-MILLION-YEAR-OLD FOSSILS

One hundred and twenty-five million years ago, in northern China and southeast Mongolia, there was a beautifully forested area where dinosaurs, birds, lizards, and fish once lived. One day, a volcano erupted and the blast killed all the creatures. The creatures were carried along with the pyroclastic flow, deposited into dry lakebeds, and then covered over with ash and debris. Scientists later discovered the site, which they call Jehol Biota, after a mythical land from Chinese folklore. Today, they are studying all the beautifully preserved fossil remains.

The Paleontological Society's Code of Fossil Collecting

1. Prior notification will be made and permission or appropriate permits will be secured from landowners or managers of private or public lands where fossils are to be collected.

2. All collections will be in compliance with federal, tribal in the case of Native American lands, state, and municipal laws and regulations applied to fossil collecting.

3. The collector(s) will make every effort to have fossil specimens of unique, rare, or exceptional value to the scientific community deposited in or sold to an appropriate institution that will provide for the care, curation, and study of the fossil material.

OLDEST DINOSAUR FOSSILS

The dinosaur named *Nyasasaurus* was leggy, long necked, and walked on two feet. It was found in Tanzania by University of Washington paleontologist Sterling Nesbitt and his team. The 243-million-year-old fossils are either the oldest known dinosaur or a really close relative. *Nyasasaurus* is about fifteen million years older than the previously known oldest dinosaur, *Eoraptor*, which was found in South America.

Make Your Own Fossil — *Activity*

All fossils began as living organisms. One day, long ago, those organisms were buried under mud or some other liquid sediment. Over time, a complex chemical process took place. In this process, the cellular structures of the organism were replaced with minerals from the water. As the water evaporated, the minerals remained, leaving behind a perfect copy of the organism in the rock. This type of fossilization is called *permineralization*. This process can take many years, but in this activity, you can simulate the process in just over a week.

MATERIALS
1 soft sponge
1 pair of scissors
1 small plastic container, like a butter tub
1 large plate
1–2 cups of sand
1 paper cup

warm water

1 1/2 cups salt—table salt or bath salt will work

1 spoon

Optional:

permanent marker

food coloring

toothpicks, brushes, or other excavating tools

METHOD

1. Using scissors, carefully cut your sponge into whatever shape you want your fossil to be. You may want to use a stencil or draw the shape on the sponge with a permanent marker. Some possible fossil shapes: a bone, a shell, a claw, a tooth, or even an entire dinosaur. Make sure that it can easily fit inside your plastic container. Set your sponge shape aside.

2. Cut two half-inch (1 cm) slits in the bottom of the plastic container. You may need to ask an adult for help with this.

3. Place the plastic container onto a large plate to catch any liquid.

4. Fill the bottom of the plastic container with sand, about half an inch (1 cm) deep. Place your sponge in the container and cover it with a layer of sand that is about three-quarters of an inch (2 cm) above the top of the sponge.

5. Mix three tablespoons warm water with three tablespoons salt. Stir until the salt is dissolved. Here's where you can add a few drops of food coloring into the mixture to make a colorful fossil.

6. Spoon the saltwater solution into the plastic container, completely covering the sponge. Do not press down or otherwise disturb the sand.

7. Place the plate and container in a warm, out-of-the-way place, where it won't be disturbed, like a windowsill.

8. Repeat steps 5 and 6 every day for seven days.

9. After day seven, wait another two days to allow your fossil to dry.

10. Carefully remove the fossilized sponge from the sand. (If the fossil is still damp, you should leave it for another day or two.) You may use toothpicks or brushes to remove the sand from the sponge. The salt has now permeated the sponge and created a delicate "fossil" for you to study!

QUESTIONS TO CONSIDER

- How does your "fossil" look different than the sponge you originally used?

- If you used food coloring in your sand mixture, how did that change the look of the sponge?

- How does your sponge differ from a real fossil?

- Could your sponge ever return to the way it was before you added salt water?

- Could a fossil return to the way it was before permineralization occurred?

In Situ Preservation

Archaeological sites that are left undisturbed or excavated and then reburied and left undisturbed are considered preserved *in situ*, which means "on site" or "in position." *In situ* preservation some-times happens to military crafts like ships and airplanes that are located underwater or buried in sediment.

It is the policy of the United States Navy to locate historic wrecks but leave them *in situ* and undisturbed. This is done whenever a site has reached a chemical and physical balance with its environ-ment. If the site is disturbed, deterioration may accelerate. If, for some reason, artifacts are removed, they must undergo immediate conservation and long-term monitoring.

Some *in situ* sites are considered burial grounds. Out of respect for the dead, they are left undisturbed. Other sites are deemed off-limits because they may contain unexploded weapons, environmental pollutants, or sensi-tive weapon systems that are best left alone.

Preserving and Protecting the Dead in Museums

Most of the research on ways to preserve artifacts happens at the Smithsonian Museum Conservation Institute. Their preserva-tion research focuses on how artifacts deteriorate. The data they collect is used to find new and better ways to store and display artifacts and minimize deterioration. They also develop and test new treatments that may help stabilize artifacts that are already deteriorating. The results of their research are shared with muse-ums around the world.

The preservation and protection of artifacts is the responsibility of every museum or institution that has them on display. The jobs within any institution may vary, but they fall under the following broad categories:

1. **Archivists** preserve, appraise, and authenticate historical documents and objects; create and maintain archives and databases; organize and classify artifacts; protect records by creating film and digital copies; direct workers who arrange, exhibit, and maintain the collections; coordinate

educational programs and promotional events like tours, workshops, lectures, or classes; and plan and carry out research projects. Most archivists have a master's degree in library science, archival science, or records management.

2. **Archive technicians** help archivists organize and maintain documents and objects. This position may require a bachelor's degree. You may also qualify for this position as an intern or as a student volunteer while earning your degree.

3. **Curators** manage the museum or institution and oversee all aspects of the collections; authenticate and acquire artifacts; and store and exhibit collections. They oversee research projects and are often involved in fundraising and publicity. Most curators specialize in a field like history, anthropology, or art. They may write grants, journal articles, and publicity materials. In large museums, there may be more than one curator. Most curators have a master's degree in a related discipline, and many have doctorates in their area of expertise.

4. **Museum technicians** help curators by preparing artifacts and setting up displays, and by cleaning and restoring objects and documents. They may also interact with the public and outside scholars by answering questions about the collection. For this position, you will need a bachelor's degree and some museum experience. Knowledge of how to prepare displays is also important.

5. **Conservators** manage, maintain, and preserve everything in a collection. They keep careful records and may conduct scientific, historical, or archaeological research on items in the collection. They restore artifacts and help treat them so they don't deteriorate. Conservators may work for a museum, but some are self-employed and work for several

institutions. This position requires a master's degree and a lot of experience. Getting into a graduate program is hard, so prepare early by volunteering or working as an intern.

Protecting Artifacts

- Most artifacts should be kept in climate-controlled locations at a constant humidity. This prevents them from becoming brittle (too dry) or moldy (too damp).

- When working with artifacts, museum curators wear white cotton gloves to keep the acid and oils from their hands from spreading to artifacts, as this could cause discoloration.

- Many artifacts can be damaged by unfiltered fluorescent light and direct sunlight. Museums are careful about what kind of lighting they use.

- Clean the mounted animals and the surrounding habitat using a soft brush. The dust is captured by a HEPA-filter vacuum cleaner and then taken to a landfill or, if arsenic was used in the taxidermy process, a toxic-waste disposal site.

- Protect the artifacts from pests through the use of sealed exhibition cases. Careful monitoring and elimination of pests once they are discovered is critical.

6

Studying the Dead

When it comes to studying the dead, most jobs fall into one of three categories: those who study bodies to determine cause of death, those who study bodies to assist in criminal investigations, and those who study the dead for research purposes. Within each of these categories, there are many job opportunities. Let's take a look at some of them.

Determining Cause of Death in Humans

When someone dies, the first question that is asked is, "Why did this person die?" For most, it's an easy answer. They died from a disease, an accident, or suddenly from a heart attack, drug overdose, blood clot, or seizure. Most people die in a hospital, where a doctor can attest to the cause of death and sign the death certificate. In these cases, the body is quickly released to the family for burial. If the family wants an autopsy, they can get one, but they'll have to pay for it.

If a person dies outside of a hospital or if the cause of death is not clear, the body is turned over to a coroner or a medical examiner for an autopsy. At an autopsy, the body is examined closely. It is cut open, samples of tissue are taken, and every organ, including the skin, is carefully inspected. The work of coroners or medical examiners can determine if a person died from a blow to the head or accidental drowning. They can discover if a person died from an overdose of drugs or heart failure. They can determine if the cause of death was crime related, and they can discover evidence on the body that may help solve that crime. There are myriad ways that they can use scientific evidence to determine cause of death.

Coroner

The job of a coroner is to determine how and why a person died. Besides performing an autopsy, coroners do the following:

- visit the death scene

- identify human remains

- supervise the transport of corpses

- operate crime scene equipment

- complete and sign death certificates

- notify next of kin

- catalog personal items of the deceased and pass them on to the next of kin

Today, coroners are public officials and are either appointed by a sheriff or county commissioners, or elected by the public. They don't need medical experience, which in some cases makes it difficult for them to determine cause of death. For more complex cases, coroners will send the corpse to a medical professional.

If you want to work as a coroner, you'll need a bachelor's degree and to take classes in biology, anatomy, forensics, and other related subjects. In many states and counties, a coroner is called a medical examiner. This means that the person is a doctor and has a license to practice medicine. To become a medical examiner, you have to go to medical school.

The Beginning of the End of Coroners?

There is a growing push in the United States to stop using coroners and start appointing medical examiners. In 2009, the National Academy of Sciences investigated the coroner system. They found that a lack of medical training, no mandatory standards for autopsies, and the absence of oversight was creating a flawed system that should be abolished.

One of the main reasons the Academy made their recommendation was to get politics out of death investigations. Some coroners are appointed by sheriffs, who give the job to a political supporter. Others are elected in county elections and voted in by people who don't understand the need for medical training. Or the position is tacked onto a sheriff's responsibilities and is not considered important when the public votes.

As death investigations require more education and skills, many believe they can no longer be conducted by people who have little or no training in the field. The downside to a shift from coroner to medical examiner is financial. Many counties and cities don't have the funds to pay a highly skilled doctor, and sometimes when they do, there often isn't a qualified person living in the area. One answer to the problem could be to share the expense and have one medical examiner oversee investigations in multiple jurisdictions.

History of Coroners

Coroners are first mentioned around 871 to 910 CE in England, during the reign of Alfred the Great. Unfortunately, there are no official records from that time, so their exact responsibilities are unknown. The job of coroner, as we know it today, dates to September 1194, when it was established during the reign of Richard the Lionheart.

At the time, sheriffs were the main law officers in each county. They were cruel and greedy and lined their own pockets with tax money collected from the people. Justiciar of the King and Archbishop of Canterbury Hubert Walter knew about their thievery and set up a network of coroners who were independent from the sheriffs. These coroners made sure that the tax money flowed into the royal coffers, bypassing the sheriffs' pockets.

Walter established the position of coroner, "the crowner," using Article 20 of the "Articles of Eyre." It stated that, "In every county of the king's realm shall be elected three knights and one clerk, to keep the pleas of the crown." Each county had three coroners and a clerk to keep the written records.

WHO GETS AN AUTOPSY? SUSPICIOUS, UNUSUAL, OR UNNATURAL DEATHS

- Homicides
- Suicides
- Accidents
- Death while in jail or prison
- Diseases that threaten public health
- Bodies to be cremated
- Bodies to be buried at sea
- Bodies transported out of state or country
- Bodies of transplant donors who died from trauma

Over time, coroners began to expand their role from "keeping the pleas," which meant watching and recording what the sheriffs did, to "holding the pleas," which meant acting as judges, trying cases, and passing sentences. This abuse of power led to the wording in the twenty-fourth chapter of the Magna Carta that states, "No sheriff, constable, coroner, or bailiff shall hold please of our Crown." This took the responsibility of judging crimes out of their hands and put it into the hands of judges.

Deputy Coroner

Deputy coroners are hired by the county. They work under a coroner or medical examiner and help determine cause of death and identify remains. As a deputy coroner, be prepared to work long hours in all weather conditions. You will be exposed to body fluids, chemicals, and horrid smells! Because of this, you should be adamant about sticking to safety procedures. This job varies by state, but may include

- photographing crime scenes

- interpreting autopsy results

- filling out death certificates

- investigating unusual or unattended deaths

- taking samples for toxicology reports

- taking custody of the body

- testifying in court about cases

- notifying next of kin

- writing technical reports

- fingerprinting corpses

- documenting traumatic wounds on corpses

Education requirements vary by state, with some states requiring a high school diploma and on-the-job training while others require an associate's degree or higher in nursing, law enforcement, medical technology, or a related field. Because this position is a law-enforcement position, deputy coroners must typically be able to pass the written, psychological, and physical tests that police officers are required to pass, as well as background checks, drug tests, and lie detector tests.

CRIME AND TRAUMA SCENE DECONTAMINATION

When investigators, coroners, paramedics, and police officers have left the scene of a crime or suicide, they don't clean up what is left behind. Families or business owners are left to clean up the mess. Unfortunately, most people don't have the necessary knowledge to do it properly. That's where crime and trauma scene decontamination (CTS Decon) teams come on the scene.

CTS Decon teams are specially trained to handle blood, bodily fluids, dangerous bacteria like anthrax, and dangerous chemicals like those used to make illegal drugs, and dispose of them properly. You don't need a degree to work on a decontamination team. Most people are trained by their employer. The pay is good, but the work is often sporadic. You need to be physically fit, so you can work many hours in a protective suit, and have a strong stomach to withstand gross scenes and strong smells.

Medical Examiner

Like coroners, medical examiners' main task is to determine cause of death and to assist in any later criminal investigation. Unlike elected coroners, they are appointed or hired for the job. They are also required to be practicing medical doctors. Although they are not specially trained for death investigations, many take extra classes in pathology (the study of disease), forensics (gathering and examining information), and other related subjects. Some may even pursue general pathology during their residency.

Morgue Technician

A morgue is where bodies are stored until they are identified and autopsied. Morgues are found in hospitals, funeral homes, and county coroner offices. Morgues often house bodies that are part of a criminal investigation or the bodies of those who died under suspicious circumstances.

Morgue technicians transport bodies, including those that are damaged or decomposed. They assist medical examiners in performing autopsies by opening the body, removing the internal organs, and taking tissue, blood, and body fluid samples. They stitch up autopsy cuts and clean the body before it is released for burial. They are in charge of keeping the morgue clean, which includes sterilizing machines, equipment, and all other surfaces.

Although you legally only need a high school diploma to be a morgue technician, most employers prefer you have at least an associate's degree in a related field. Being a morgue technician is considered an entry-level job and will help you work your way up to a higher position. It is important that you are a caring and compassionate person and that you handle all aspects of caring for the deceased with dignity and respect.

Morgue Security

Morgue security guards are responsible for making sure only people legally allowed to be in the morgue are there. Usually this position requires a high school degree and is similar to other security jobs. However, in some cases, morgue security is handled by law enforcement.

Morgue security is crucial when the body is part of a criminal investigation. It is important that the body not be disturbed, as this may taint the evidence in the case. Even when the body isn't part of a criminal investigation, morgues sometimes need security guards. They are there to provide a safe work environment for morgue staff and protect them from angry or distraught family members of the deceased. They also guard famous or infamous bodies from those who want to see, touch, or damage them.

Morgue Attendant/Assistant

Morgue attendants help with the daily work in a morgue. They may log in a corpse, weigh and measure it, help with and clean up after autopsies, and file paperwork that allows the body to be released.

Assisting in Criminal Investigations

When a death is caused by the actions of another person, it is called *murder*. Whether the death happened yesterday or a hundred years ago, if the perpetrator is still living, he or she can be prosecuted and sent to prison. Helping in the investigation of these crimes is a host of professionals who are dedicated to finding justice for the victim.

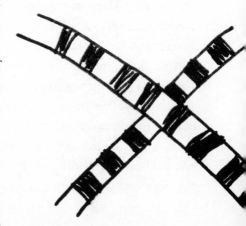

DEFINITIONS OF MURDER UNDER THE LAW

- **First degree/capital murder**—the most serious offense. The crime was planned in advance and the offender was thinking clearly when he or she killed another person

- **Second degree murder**—intentionally killing someone without planning it in advance, usually happens because of jealousy and anger

- **Felony murder**—a murder that happens during the process of a felony crime, like killing a bystander while robbing a bank

- **Involuntary manslaughter**—unintentionally killing another without forethought, like a drunk driver who hits and kills a pedestrian

- **Voluntary manslaughter**—when one person kills another when provoked by anger or in self-defense

Forensics and Forensic?

Today, there is a lot of confusion over the use of these two words. *Forensics* is a very old word, dating back hundreds of years to the ancient Greeks. *Forensics*, with an *s*, is the art and study of formal argument and debate by using science and technology to investigate and establish facts in criminal or civil courts of law. It is a skill honed by lawyers, judges, politicians, and others in careers where they regularly need to communicate a position before a judge, jury, or group of people.

Recently, the word has evolved into a descriptive word that is added to any scientist whose career is focused on solving crimes. Adding the word *forensic*, without an *s*, means that the person is using science and technology to investigate and establish facts in cases that might be tried in criminal or civil courts of law.

Forensic Pathologist

Forensic pathologists are medical doctors who take their medical training one step further. They graduate from medical school, finish their two- or three-year residency, and then do another year of residency in forensic pathology. This is usually done under the supervision of a certified medical examiner. Forensic pathologists may work as medical examiners for city, county, or state governments, or in hospitals or medical schools. They may also work in private practice or with a group performing autopsies for governments, lawyers, or at the request of the deceased's family.

Besides autopsies, forensic pathologists and other forensic scientists collect data from the dead to try and help the living. They may investigate new diseases or genetic causes of death. They also research trends in deaths to keep governments and medical professionals informed and to educate the public.

Forensic Archaeologist

Forensic archaeologists use all the tools and techniques of archaeologists to help in the investigation of a crime. Their job is to help in the search for a burial site, interpret what has happened at the burial site, and carefully record and recover the remains and other evidence at the site.

Forensic archaeologists or other forensic scientists help identify victims and aid in the investigation of crimes. They also help recover and identify remains in mass death events like airplane crashes or newly discovered mass burial sites, like those found after or during a war.

Osteologist/Bioarchaeologist

Osteologists study human bones and use their knowledge of the human skeleton in the recovery and identification of human remains. They may assist in criminal investigations by interpreting damage to the bones and establishing cause of death.

Bioarchaeologists study the bones of the long dead to understand lifespans, diseases, and causes of death in ancient times. They also study the ancient dead to establish human evolutionary lineage. The proper collection and study of human bones can provide valuable information about past societies, including ethnic origins, sex, age, stature (which tells whether or not a group of people were well nourished), and some of the diseases that hurt or killed them.

How skeletons reveal information:

- Femur—the length of this bone helps determine the height of the individual.

- Skull—its size and shape are used to determine ethnicity.

- Skull and pelvis—different shapes identify male or female; this is less accurate when dealing with the bones of children.

- All bones—since they change with age, indicators like bone development, wear and tear on joint bones, and tooth growth can help establish age. Damage to bones can identify trauma or disease.

ALEXIS GRAY, PhD, FORENSIC ANTHROPOLOGIST
SAN BERNARDINO COUNTY, CALIFORNIA

When did you first become interested in anthropology and decide to make it the focus of your career?
I was in my second year of college. I had been a marine biology major, but I found out while working for a marine lab that I actually hated fish and having wet feet every day. I took

an anthropology course and loved it. I didn't know for sure what branch of the discipline I wanted to pursue, but I knew anthropology was the right field for me.

The important part is that until I found the right career path, I was a C student. I thought I was dumb, because math and I didn't get along. I wanted to be a doctor, but I was afraid I simply wasn't smart enough. It turns out that I was wrong. I just hadn't matured to a level where I was ready to tackle math and focus on my studies. It took me until I was twenty years old to pass a math course! But by the time I was twenty-five, I was using statistics daily and loving it.

What education/work path did you take to get where you are today?
I had a strong background in zoology and physiology, so I coupled them with anthropology to earn my bachelor's degree. I went on to earn a master's in human osteology and then a PhD in anthropology.

From start to finish, it took me eighteen years to complete all my studies: four years in community college, two and a half years in a four-year institution, two and a half years for my master's, and eight years for my PhD. I could have earned my degrees faster, but I had to go a bit slower because I had a child, and later became a single mom.

How did you end up working for the San Bernardino County Sheriff's Department as a forensic scientist?
My mentor recommended me for the position, but I volunteered for several years before it became a paying job.

Describe what a forensic anthropologist's job is like.
As a forensic scientist, I help law enforcement identify human remains, and I help with specialized evidence recovery using my archaeology training.

Working as a forensic anthropologist (FA) isn't a daily job. Most FAs work on contract, as needed. If it's a day with a case, I'll go to the scene and do the recovery. That may entail mapping a scatter on the surface or digging up a body using archaeological techniques.

On an autopsy day, I'll examine the body with the pathologist, taking about 175 measurements, hopefully in under half an hour, and taking about fifty pictures. If there is time and the pathologist approves, I clean the body of all soft tissue. That can take an entire day if I do it the quick way, or several days over a six-month period if I do it the gentle way. The job is really tough. Especially taking someone's face off. The face is their last bit of human identity, and removing it can be very emotionally difficult. If I have students present, I lose some of them during that part. Some students only want to do the fun investigations, not the smelly scrubbing and cutting of rotten flesh. But it's part of the job.

Then the body is preserved and protected until it is identified. After the autopsy, a report must be filed. A standard report, with no complicated issues, takes about six hours to produce. During that six hours, I do statistical analysis and describe the process of recovery and autopsy. I read journal articles to make sure my citations are correct. Sometimes I have to draw maps, which take a couple additional hours to complete.

I'm not paid by the hour. I'm paid by the case. Sometimes that's great, a few minutes comparing x-rays to make an identification, but sometimes I spend about a hundred hours on a single case. Some years I have been needed a lot. I had eleven cases in the last two months. But last year, I had only seven for the whole year. However, at least once a week, I'm asked to determine if a bone is human or not (it's usually not), so at least I touch FA work each week. On the weekend, I read journals and grade papers. Exciting, no? What do I do with the rest of my time? I teach classes. Most FAs are also college professors.

Why is this work important to you?

Each time I work, I know I have a chance to make a difference by offering a family member closure.

Unfortunately, part of the perceived duties of this job is being "Dr. Death" to your friends and family. Every time someone dies who is even remotely connected to me, I get a phone call asking for help. Can I speed up the autopsy? Can I help with or arrange the funeral? I have been asked to do some horrific things by my friends who have suffered tragic losses. I have done them, because who else will, but it takes a very serious toll on me. Somehow people think I'm supposed to be above it all, that I'm never supposed to feel the passing, and just do my job. That isn't always possible.

Bones is a much-loved television series, and you've consulted with the writers on that show. What was it like working with them?

I consulted with them because I believe that real science is better than fake TV science and much more interesting. Ultimately, they used a story I told them from some of my early years in school. It had nothing to do with forensic science, but it was really cool hearing them tell my jokes! I also advised them on their sets, but I don't believe the advice was ever taken.

As a teacher and a forensic scientist, what do you like most about your jobs?

As a teacher, I enjoy encouraging critical-thinking skills. Even if my students don't remember the specific material, if I can teach them how to reason through a problem and get them to ask "Why?" or "How do you know that?" I have succeeded. I feel that I've changed a lot of lives for the better, that I really make a difference.

As a forensic scientist, it is all about closure and solving the puzzle. The real life of a forensic scientist is not glamorous and can be personally costly. It is not romantic, but I do it because it is necessary and I would want someone to do it for me. It is about being a good community member and a good citizen.

What advice would you give a young person who is interested in becoming a forensic scientist?
I wouldn't recommend my particular field because the competition is ridiculous—less than a hundred of us working in the country with thousands of us with degrees. I would say there are many ways to contribute. Forensic nursing is very important, as is forensic pathology. With forensic nursing, you may even have a chance to help someone stay alive. Be a doctor, be a nurse, be a counselor. Make an impact on the living.

Volunteer where you can. Try the actual job. Have a backup plan. The forensic science field is as saturated as Hollywood is with actors. Look at job descriptions for jobs you want and talk to people, honestly, about what it is they actually do. Consider the income. Being poor sounds super romantic when you are being supported by your parents, but in reality it's not fun. When you have to decide between shoes for your kid and a week's worth of ramen noodles, you might question your choice.

What do you see as future trends in forensic science?
As technology improves, anything is possible. Some of our technology is driven by science fiction, so I have hopes that room scanners and 3-D holographic images will someday become real. Then we will do what they say we already can do on television. As far as careers, obviously, forensic data (computer) reconstruction and internet security are the way to go.

Forensic Photographers

Forensic photographers take pictures of accidents and crime scenes, including the victims and the surrounding area. They must be highly skilled and detail oriented because their work is often relied upon in court cases.

You don't need a college degree to become a forensic photographer. However, this area is highly competitive because of the popularity of crime shows on television. What you need to know is that it isn't a glamorous job. You must be willing to work in all kinds of weather, in high-stress situations, and in circumstances that are often difficult to witness. Your work must be accurate every time.

If you want to become a forensic photographer, start as a great photographer. Learn to view scenes objectively and capture images that are clear, unbiased, and accurate. After that, there are classes available at local colleges and online. Once you are ready to find a job, research your local police departments and sheriff's offices to understand their hiring requirements.

Forensic Entomologist

Forensic entomologists study insects that are used as evidence in criminal or civil court cases. They study entomology in college, earning a bachelor's, master's, and sometimes a doctoral degree, and then focus their career on the bugs that interact with the dead. They help police understand and document what happened to a body after death.

Here's what happens:

Shortly after death, microorganisms like fungi and bacteria start the decomposition process. This can happen fast or slow, depending on weather conditions. If it is hot and humid, the body decomposes faster than if it is cool and dry. The speed of decomposition is also influenced by whether or not the body was buried, how much fat is on the body, and whether or not it was clothed.

Within a few hours, insects follow the smell of decaying flesh, find the corpse, and begin to eat and reproduce. These insects, called *carrion insects*, live their entire lives on decaying flesh. When one body is completely decomposed, the adults fly to the next closest body, lay their eggs, and live out their lives there. The study of

their life cycles is how forensic ento-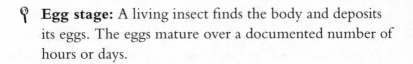
mologists accurately determine how
long a person has been dead.

There are three stages that an
insect goes through while living in a dead body.

- **Egg stage:** A living insect finds the body and deposits its eggs. The eggs mature over a documented number of hours or days.

- **Larval stage:** The egg matures and a small, white larva emerges. The larva grows while feeding on the dead flesh. It grows for a documented number of days before moving on to the final stage.

- **Pupal stage:** The transition stage where a larva transforms into a winged adult.

There are five stages that a body goes through while decomposing. Each step attracts different kinds of flesh-eating bugs.

- **Fresh (0 to 4 days):** The body cools, and bacteria start to break down tissue. This produces gas and emits a smell that attracts insects. Flies arrive and feed on body fluids. The most common are blowflies, and they offer the most accurate estimation of time of death.

- **Putrefaction (4 to 10 days):** The gas causes the body to bloat. Bacteria in the colon move into the vascular system, and the face and abdomen begin to swell. Skin breaks down and falls away, turning from green to brown. Flesh flies and houseflies love the semi-liquid environment of this stage.

- **Black putrefaction (10 to 20 days):** The body bursts, the gases escape, and the internal organs are infested with insects. By the end of this stage, the organs are a chunky liquid. Cheese flies and coffin flies are abundant at this stage.

- **Butyric fermentation (20 to 50 days):** The corpse begins to dry out and look like a mummy. The smell caused by the feasting bacteria begins to disappear. Beetles, like the hide beetle and carcass beetle, appear and devour the dry skin and muscles. There may also be some varieties of flies, as well as moths and mites, on the corpse.

- **Dry decay to skeletonization (50 days to 1 year):** All the tissue rots away. The bones fall apart and form a pile or are scattered by predators.

WORKING STIFF *profile*

Dr. Tim Huntington, Board Certified Forensic Entomologist
Associate Professor of Biology and Criminal Justice, Concordia University
Seward, Nebraska

When did you first become interested in entomology and decide to make it the focus of your career?
I was a junior in college, and I was looking for a research topic for my field ecology course. I remembered that my high school biology teacher had told me a little about forensic entomology, so I thought I would try doing a project on that subject. I found out that I absolutely loved it! I ended up doing more advanced research my senior year, and the more I learned about insects, the more I found that I liked them. They really are pretty amazing animals.

What education/work path did you take to get where you are today, including what you did as a teenager?

I would say that it all started when I was sixteen, when I started working for a mortuary service back in Indianapolis. My job was doing removals, which is picking up bodies from where they died and transporting them to funeral homes. I worked there for five years, mostly over school breaks and weekends since I had to be on call twenty-four hours a day.

I went to Concordia University in Nebraska, where I am now a professor, for my undergraduate degree in biology. Then I spent the next six years at the University of Nebraska-Lincoln, where I got my master's degree and PhD in entomology.

You have worked with law enforcement on over one hundred death cases. What do you do with the bugs that law enforcement finds? And what do they tell you about the scene of a crime or a death?

The insects that are most important to me are the ones that feed on the body, which are primarily the maggots from blow-flies. Once someone dies, the body becomes a valuable food source for a whole host of insects. And because these insects are attracted to dead people from the moment that they die, they are very useful in estimating how long that person has been dead.

For example, if the maggots on a body are about ten days old, that means the person has been dead for at least that same ten days. By knowing about the habits of the flies that laid their eggs on the body, you can narrow things down even more, until you're left with an estimated time since death. Most of the cases that I'm involved with have questions related to the time of death. The insects on the body and at the scene provide some of the best means of answering those questions.

I also use insects to provide information about where someone died, how they died, and sometimes even to identify potential suspects.

What fascinates you the most about your entomology work, and why is it important to you?

Once you know about the interaction between dead bodies and the organisms that feed on them, everything becomes very predictable. Sometimes I'm amazed about the things I'm able to say about a death investigation or the predictions I'm able to make when doing a study.

Investigators are often shocked when I give them my report. They are amazed by how closely it matches what they turned up during their investigation, especially because my work was done independently from theirs.

My work is important to me as a scientist because I'm able to help figure out what really happened at a scene. I tell investigators and attorneys that I don't know whether my analysis will help them or not, but it will uncover the truth. The insects don't lie. They don't have a stake in the outcome of the investigation. I just tell people what the insects are saying, so there isn't any pressure on me to say one thing or another.

You are also interested in carrion ecology (the study of decaying flesh). Explain what that includes and why it's important to your work.

Carrion ecology is the study of interactions between organisms and dead animals (including humans). When anything dies, it is eaten by *something*. Whether the animal is eaten by bacteria, fungi, invertebrates, or vertebrates, it will be eaten. That includes all of us too! So carrion ecology is the basis for the study of decomposition. As a forensic entomologist, I spend a lot of time studying the portion that involves insects. But because all the other organisms that are eating a body are interacting with the insects, it is vital for me to understand those aspects as well.

What advice would you give a young person who is interested in becoming an entomologist?

Spend time outside and observe the world around you. It is so amazing how much you actually learn when you just watch things happening in nature. Catch some insects or take some pictures, and spend time with your family and friends while you're at it. Eventually people will pay you to do the same thing!

What do you see as future trends in forensic entomology?

There is a gradual increase in the number of cases that use insects as evidence from death investigations, which is great. A lot of investigators have historically been unaware that insects can be helpful when looking at a body, so the evidence was lost. As we do a better job of educating people on the roles that insects have in decomposition, their value is being recognized more frequently.

THE FIRST FORENSIC ENTOMOLOGIST

The story of forensic entomology begins over eight hundred years ago in a small Chinese village. One very hot day, several farmers were walking home from their fields. Along the way, they discovered the hacked body of a neighbor lying beside the road.

The local death inspector was called in, and he began an investigation. After careful thought, he decided that the farmer wasn't killed by bandits, but by someone who hated him. Bandits kill for money, but the dead farmer's valuables were untouched.

After talking to the dead man's wife and finding no known enemies, the inspector ordered everyone in the village to bring their scythes to the town square. Within an hour, there were seventy or eighty scythes lying on the ground before him. Because of the heat, flies began to gather around one scythe, attracted to the faint smell of blood. The owner of the fly-infested scythe, when faced with the evidence, confessed. He had murdered the farmer because the farmer owed him money.

This story was first recorded by a Chinese death investigator named Sung Tz'u in his book titled *The Washing Away of Wrongs*, which was written in 1235 CE.

FRESH MEAT
profile

CALEB SEEKINS, BUG COLLECTOR
RYAN MIDDLE SCHOOL
FAIRBANKS, ALASKA
AGE: 12

Most kids are interested in bugs. They are amazing creatures. When did you first discover a love for creepy, crawly insects?
My mom says that I started going after insects when I was a toddler, so I guess I was interested in them since then.

Do you have a collection of insects?
I don't have a collection of insects, because I didn't have a way to store them. I would put them in jars, containers, or paper cups, but they would always be let loose, knocked over, and damaged or thrown away.

This year I was given a nice box to store my insects. We still need to buy foam to put inside it, but entomologist Derek Sikes gave me a set of his pinning needles so that they won't slip away. I have two beetles for it.

How did you find the rare beetle that is now in the University of Alaska's collection?
My mom spotted it first, when she was outside by her greenhouse. She called to me to see if it was the same kind of beetle that I had found a year before. By the time that I got to where she was, she had lost where the beetle was. I searched the ground and around her greenhouse until I spotted him. It was the same beetle that I had seen a year before. I told my mom to get a container so we could capture it.

How did you know that it was different from other beetles and should be sent to the museum?
About a year before, we had a barbecue at our house. I started telling my mom about this beetle that was rainbow colored. She thought I was making it up, but as I described it, Mr. Sikes became excited and pulled out a specimen jar—he apparently keeps them with him—and wanted me to show him where I found the beetle, so he could collect it and put it in the collection at the library. He said that it was an unusual find, as they are pretty rare in our area.

We went out to where I originally found my rainbow beetle, but we couldn't find it. We spent an hour looking around at different insects on felled trees. Mr. Sikes told us the name of the beetle and that it's commonly referred to as a rainbow beetle because it looks like a rainbow on its back.

A year later, when my mom was outside, she briefly saw that rainbow on an insect. She remembered that Mr. Sikes wanted to collect one. That's why she called me, because I'm the one who saw it. Once I found the beetle, I told her that this was the rainbow beetle. She suggested we contact Mr. Sikes to see if he wanted it for his collection at the university because he had said it was rare.

What was it like taking a rare beetle to the University of Alaska Museum of the North and meeting entomologist Dr. Derek Sikes?

I had met him before. My mom took me to the museum one year on Halloween. The museum opens its doors and lets the kids come in and see the different labs and meet the professors. The beetle is rare in our area. Its scientific name is *Carabus vietinghoffi*.

You were named a "collector" at the museum. What does that mean?

It means I collected a bug. When we gave them the beetle, I asked if it would say "collected by Caleb Seekins" on the label. They said it would. Cool for a kid!

Besides your beetle, what insects fascinate you and why?

I have raised honeybees with my mom for the last three years. Honeybees are really important. They are pollinators and make us honey. We eat the honey to help with our allergies.

I also like mosquitos. I like how they can take blood from creatures, and they use a chemical to stop the bleeding. I don't like being bitten by them, but how they do it is interesting.

Where do you see yourself in ten years?

Insects still interest me, but I like other things too, now that I'm older. I like robotics a lot, so I think I will be studying computer programming in college.

Preserving Insects

The earth is filled with insects! According to most estimates, there are over nine hundred thousand known species of insects living today. The number of unknown species is thought to range anywhere from two to thirty million. In the United States, there are about ninety-one thousand described species and seventy-three thousand undescribed.

In order to keep track and describe each insect, entomologists collect specimens and preserve them for study and comparison. Insects are usually preserved by drying them out, mounting them on a board using a long, sharp pin, and protecting them in a glass-covered case.

Insects are identified by class, order, family, genus, and then species. All insects belong to the class Insecta. Within this class, there are thirty orders. In the United States, most insects fall into four orders: beetles (*Coleoptera*); flies (*Diptera*); ants, bees, and wasps (*Hymenoptera*); and moths and butterflies (*Lepidoptera*).

It is important to know where your insect ranks within these classifications, so you can easily identify it, compare it with others of the same species, and talk intelligently with other collectors.

Start an Insect Collection — Activity

Collecting insects can be a great way to study them. Collecting, drying, and mounting insects is easy and inexpensive. Reminder: Some insects bite or sting. Be careful when you are handling them. Adult supervision is recommended when collecting some insects because a bite or sting may cause an allergic reaction.

MATERIALS
1 net (optional)
2 pint jars, clean and with air-tight lids
10 cotton balls
rubbing alcohol or acetone (fingernail polish remover)

1 piece of cardboard, small enough to fit inside your jar
1 pair of scissors
masking tape
1 pair of tweezers
1 one-inch-thick piece of hard foam,
  big enough for your bug
insect pins or long sewing pins
1 index card
1 permanent marker
1 storage container
moth ball flakes

STEP ONE: CATCHING YOUR INSECT

Insects can be found almost anywhere—under rocks, on plants, and flying through the air. Sweep your net through a patch of tall grass. After a few tries, you'll probably catch a moth, butterfly, or other flying bug. If the net doesn't work, look under something; you'll probably find ants, beetles, or centipedes. Once you've chosen the insect you want to preserve, put it in one of the pint jars.

STEP TWO: KILLING YOUR INSECT

After you've caught your insect and safely put it in a jar, it's time to carefully kill it.

- Put some fingernail polish remover on each cotton ball, and drop them into the other glass jar. Be sure there is no standing liquid because it may damage your insect.

- Using your scissors, punch four small holes in the piece of cardboard. Place the piece of cardboard into the jar so it lies horizontally, resting over the cotton balls. This will protect your specimen from getting wet or damaged, but will still allow the fumes from the nail polish remover to permeate the jar.

- Using your tweezers, gently pick up the bug and place it on the cardboard. If your insect is flying, tap the jar it is in, knocking it to the bottom. Then quickly remove the lid and turn the jar over, matching its opening with the opening of your killing jar. Tap again until the bug drops into the killing jar.

- Tightly seal the lid on the killing jar.

- Wait several hours for your insect to die.

STEP THREE: DRYING YOUR INSECT

Now that your insect is dead, it's time to pin and dry it. You should always try to pin your insect within a couple of hours of killing it. If you wait too long, the insect will become brittle and break.

- Using your tweezers, gently remove your insect from the killing jar and place it on the piece of foam.

- Push the pin through the thickest section of the body. Make sure you keep the pin straight, or your bug will be mounted at an angle. Push the pin into the foam until the insect's body is lying flat on the foam and there is about a quarter of the pin left above the insect. This extra space allows for easier handling.

- Adjust the wings and legs of your insect into the positions where you want them to remain. Pin them in this position, being very careful with the delicate wings and legs.

- Write up a label using an index card and permanent marker. Your label should state the name of the insect, where it was collected (county, state, park), habitat information (forest, field, marsh), the date it was collected, and the name of the collector. Pin the label near the insect for easy identification.

ϙ Allow the insect to dry for five to seven days.

STEP FOUR: PRESERVING YOUR INSECT

Insects must be kept in a special storage box if they are going to last. These boxes have a soft bottom to make it easier to pin insects, and are covered with a plate of glass or plexiglass to allow for viewing. Without a protective case, insects will become covered in dust, have parts broken off, or will be completely destroyed in a short amount of time. You can buy a storage box online or make one.

ϙ Remove the pin from the foam, being careful to keep the insect intact.

ϙ Poke the pin through your label, so the bug is hovering above it.

ϙ Firmly push the pin into the bottom of the storage box. This should be coated with some foam-like substance that will allow it to be securely mounted.

Protect your insect from other insects and mold by placing a few flakes from a mothball in the storage box. Mothballs are made using chemicals that can make you sick. Be sure to wear gloves or wash your hands after handling them.

Congratulations! You have mounted your first insect. Remember, practice makes perfect. The more insects you collect and preserve, the better they will look.

FIVE LARGEST BUG COLLECTIONS IN THE UNITED STATES

1. **The United States National Entomological Collection** at the Smithsonian National Museum of Natural History in Washington, DC. It's the second-largest collection in the world, with over thirty-five million specimens representing about 60 percent of the world's known insect families.

2. **American Museum of Natural History's Division of Invertebrate Zoology** in New York City, New York. The collection has about twenty-four million specimens from about five hundred thousand species.

3. **California Academy of Sciences' Department of Entomology** in San Francisco. The collection has over ten million specimens from about 250,000 species.

4. **The Chicago Field Museum's Division of Insects** in Illinois. The collection has 4.1 million pinned specimens and 8.3 million preserved in alcohol or on microscope slides.

5. The Cornell University Insect Collection in Ithaca, New York. The collection has about seven million specimens from about two hundred thousand species, or roughly 20 percent of the world's known insects.

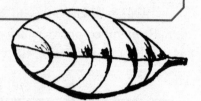

7

Remembering the Dead

Not all jobs working with the dead are focused on finding, caring for, preserving, or studying dead people, animals, or plants. Some jobs center on remembering the dead.

There are people who work in cemeteries, where the dead are laid to rest and remembered with monuments, tombstones, or plaques. Historians remember and study the dead who lived within a given society, century, or decade. They may study Russian royal families, the poor during the Black Plague, or Antebellum slaves. Historians also analyze past lives, from prehistory through the twentieth century, and interpret what people's lives were like and how they impacted human history. Genealogists study past lives and record each individual who is part of a family, so future generations will remember them.

Cemeteries

Cemeteries can be either public or private. A public cemetery is used by the community, neighborhood, or a church. It may be privately owned and managed, but must be open to the public for the burial of their dead. A private cemetery or a family burying ground is used by a family or a small number of people in a community. There are no spaces sold to the public, and burial in it is usually restricted to a group of people who are related by blood or marriage.

Within a cemetery, there are two places where bodies are buried. They can be placed in the ground and marked with a headstone, or put in a mausoleum or burial chamber. A mausoleum is a building where caskets are put in aboveground vaults and marked with a memorial plaque. If a person is cremated, the burial options are the same, in the ground or in a mausoleum.

DEAD VOCABULARY

Taphophilia (taf-o-feel-ee-uh) is an abnormal interest in funerals, graves, and cemeteries.

Thanatophobia (than-uh-tuh-foe-bee-uh) is the fear of death.

Necrophobia (nek-ruh-foe-bee-uh) is the fear of corpses.

Phasmophobia (fas-muh-foe-bee-uh) is the fear of ghosts.

Coimetrophobia (coy-met-ruh-foe-bee-uh) is the fear of cemeteries.

Kinemortophobia (kin-uh-mort-uh-foe-bee-uh) is the fear of zombies.

FIVE WELL-KNOWN CEMETERIES

Arlington National Cemetery, Arlington, Virginia
Dead service members from all four branches of the United States military are buried here. This cemetery is the home of the Tomb of the Unknowns or Tomb of the Unknown Soldier (it has never been officially named), in which are buried the unidentified remains of one serviceman from World War I, World War II, and the Korean War. There are no unknown remains from Vietnam or either of the Gulf Wars.

Forest Lawn Memorial Park, Los Angeles, California
Hollywood Hills and Glendale are the two cemeteries included in Forest Lawn Memorial Park. Many famous people are buried here including Walt Disney, Jimmy Stewart, and Liberace. The park contains many pieces of art, like a stained-glass replica of *The Last Supper* and a replica of Old North Church in Boston.

Gettysburg National Cemetery, Gettysburg, Pennsylvania
Gettysburg National Cemetery is the final resting place of more than 3,500 Union soldiers who fought and died in the Battle of Gettysburg in June 1863. There are many monuments in the park dedicated to the soldiers who died in that Civil War battle.

Lafayette Cemetery No. 1, New Orleans, Louisiana
This cemetery lies below sea level, so uses aboveground vaults that often hold more than one person from a family. The cemetery is often referred to as a "city of the dead" because the vaults make the cemetery look like a bleached-white city block. The famous voodoo practitioner Marie Laveau is buried here.

Sleepy Hollow Cemetery, Sleepy Hollow, New York
This cemetery is the site of Washington Irving's famous spooky tale "The Legend of Sleepy Hollow." Irving is buried here, as well as Andrew Carnegie and William Rockefeller.

FLAVOR GRAVEYARD

Whenever one of Ben & Jerry's Ice Cream flavors is discontinued because of poor sales, it is buried in the Flavor Graveyard in Waterbury, Vermont. Each dead flavor is given a headstone with its name, dates of production, and a brief memorial poem engraved on it.

Gravedigger

Before burial, gravediggers are responsible for digging a hole at the grave site, placing in a concrete vault, and setting in place the coffin-lowering mechanism. After the burial ceremony, they lower the coffin into the vault, set the vault cover, and backfill the soil. Gravediggers may also set up canopies and chairs, and position headstones. Depending on the cemetery, this position can be filled by part-time, unskilled laborers, or it can be a full-time career if combined with lawn and garden maintenance.

Groundskeeper

The groundskeeper maintains the cemetery grounds. This person is responsible for mowing and edging the lawn, as well as trimming and caring for the trees and plants. Groundskeepers sometimes have the job of gravedigger, and set up and complete burials and cremations. Most grounds-keeping jobs only require a high school diploma.

Alternatives to Traditional Burials

Over the years, people have looked for unique ways to say their final good-byes. The famous actress Elizabeth Taylor knew that arriving at her funeral would be her final grand entrance. She amused her mourning family and friends by requesting that her casket arrive fifteen minutes late. It was announced, "She even wanted to be late for her own funeral!"

Some people don't want to be buried in a cemetery. There are a number of other ways they can be buried or have their remains disposed. Keep in mind that with each of these unique burial ideas, there are jobs associated with them. Here are a few interesting ways to bid this world a final *adieu*:

1. **A green burial**—return to dust. The body is not embalmed. It is placed in a biodegradable pine box or a shroud and buried in a hand-dug grave, usually beneath a tree. Some people even buy a coffin in advance and use it as a coffee table or a bookshelf until it's needed.

2. **Burial at sea**—become a sunken treasure. Burial at sea is legal in the United States. Bodies are taken at least three nautical miles (3.5 miles/5.6 kilometers) from land, in waters that are at least six hundred feet (183 meters) deep. The coffin or shroud is weighted so it and the body will sink to the sea floor and stay there. Cremated remains can also be scattered at sea.

3. **Human DNA trees**—become a living memorial. Human DNA is put into a tree's DNA. The result is a normal-looking tree, but the DNA of the deceased is preserved within it. Although this process is not available right now, you may see it in the near future as an environmentally friendly way of memorializing a dead loved one.

4. **Fireworks funerals**—go out with a bang. The cremains are put into specially designed fireworks and shot into the air in a spectacular light display, and the released cremains float away in the wind.

5. **Cremation art**—hang out with loved ones. The ashes are mixed with paint and used to create a unique piece of art. This can be done by a professional artist or by a member of the family. Not all of the cremains are used, so what's left can be buried, scattered, or kept in an urn.

6. **Reef burial**—sleep with the fishes. The ashes of a loved one are mixed with concrete and used to build reefs at sea. Seen as a peaceful way to be buried, this process also provides a benefit to the environment by being a home for marine life.

7. **Space burials**—become a shooting star. The cremains are placed in small capsules, carried into space aboard a spacecraft, and released into space. The capsule orbits the earth for a few months and then burns up as it falls and reenters the atmosphere.

8. **Memorial diamonds**—set in stone. Carbon is extracted from the cremated remains and turned into a diamond through the use of extreme pressure and heat. The diamonds can be put into jewelry or set in a variety of memorial objects.

Pet Cemeteries

The first pet cemetery in the United States was the Hartsdale Pet Cemetery in New York. It opened in 1896 and is now the resting place of over eighty thousand animals. It is also home to a fifty-ton, aboveground mausoleum for two spaniels and to the War Dog Memorial, which honors military dogs for their service to our nation.

Pet cemeteries are privately owned by either an individual or a corporation. They can be on their own land or part of a human cemetery. They are less regulated than human cemeteries, but some states are beginning to establish burial guidelines.

According to the *Bloomberg Business Review*, there are more than seven hundred pet death care facilities in the United States, ranging from pet cemeteries and crematories to pet memorial makers. The pet death care business is growing too. The Pet Loss Professionals Alliance estimates that 1.9 million pets were given professional death care services in 2012, with about twenty-one thousand of those being burials, and the rest cremations.

Monuments to the Dead

Since before recorded history, humans have searched for ways to remember their dead. The oldest-known monuments date to 4510 BCE and were found on the Iberian Peninsula. Around that same time, the Carnac stones in Brittany were also erected.

The ways that we have tried to remember our dead are as varied as the individuals we wish to honor. From the earliest stone monuments to today's online memorials, each generation tries to find new and unique ways to remember their dead.

There are thousands of monuments in the United States, like the San Jacinto Monument in Texas—it stands 567 feet tall and is dedicated to those who fought for Texas's independence from Mexico—or the David Berger National Memorial in Ohio—a sculpture dedicated to Berger and ten other members of the Israeli Olympic Team who died during the 1972 Olympic Games in Munich, Germany.

Some of these monuments are cared for by the National Park Service (NPS), a bureau of the Department of the Interior. The NPS oversees 27,000 historic structures and 2,461 National Historic Landmarks. They employ over twenty-thousand people, from archaeologists to landscape mechanics, all dedicated to protecting the cultural resources of the United States.

In addition to the NPS, there are state agencies and nonprofit organizations that manage some historic monuments. The San Jacinto Monument mentioned above is maintained by the nonprofit San Jacinto Museum of History Association and the Texas State Parks and Wildlife Commission.

Private organizations also work to maintain memorials. They are typically local groups that want to protect a piece of local history, especially if the place is not protected by the NPS or a state organization. One example is the Pittock Mansion Society in Portland, Oregon. They work to preserve the home of Henry and Georgiana Pittock as a memorial to their contributions to Portland and its people.

PROTECTING THE WORLD'S TREASURES

The United States military has a small group of archaeologists and historians who map out where cultural treasures, including historical sites, artwork, and important monuments, are located around the world. Known as *Monuments Men* (and women), their expertise is used by the military in an effort to avoid destroying a nation's cultural resources during a time of conflict.

This program began during World War II, when a group of three hundred officers from the Allied Forces secretly saved millions of pieces of artwork and created maps of archaeological sites so the allies could avoid them when bombing an area.

The idea of protecting every nation's historical treasures, no matter how intense the fighting, was written into the 1954 Hague Convention. It requires that all signers of the treaty agree to provide military specialists to help protect cultural property. More recently, these men and women worked during the Second Gulf War to try and protect the cultural treasures of Iraq, an ancient area known as the cradle of civilization.

Online Memorials

An online memorial is a website that provides a place for the deceased's loved ones to share pictures and memories and come to grieve and comfort one another. These memorials can remain online forever or be posted for a specific period of time. The site may include memorial service information and links to memorial funds or charities.

People who work for these sites don't deal directly with the dead, but they provide a way for the living to remember the dead. Online memorial companies look for people with strong business and online advertising skills. Their employees must know how to attract customers to their sites and know how to effectively communicate with coworkers, business partners, and customers. College courses in business, communications, and web programming will help you succeed in this field.

Historian

Historians study the past. They research eras of human history, analyze events, and then interpret what happened and why. To succeed at being a historian, you need to love searching through old documents and photographs, and finding ways to communicate your findings to others through published papers, presentations, or teaching. When conducting research, there may be a lot of travel. Working as a historian will require a bachelor's degree and for some jobs a master's degree or a doctorate.

Where Historians Work

- Archives

- Colleges and universities
  (PhD required)

- Consulting firms

- Foundations and nonprofit organizations

- Government agencies: US Department of State Office of the Historian, National Park Service, etc.

- Historic sites

- Historical societies

- Lawyers' offices

- Legislative staff

- Libraries

- Museums

- Newspapers and magazines

- Research organizations

- Schools: elementary, secondary, and high school

What Historians Do

- Advocate for preservation of historic documents, artifacts, and sites

- Edit documents

- Work to preserve historic sites

- Litigation research

- Manage cultural resources

- Manage information

- Research

- Write articles, books, and reports

- Work on documentaries and films

- Work on teaching materials and multimedia presentations

There are three skills that every historian must acquire to succeed. First, learn your native language very well. Have a strong vocabulary so you can read and understand professional documents. Know how to write so others can understand what you are trying to say. Write in an organized and cohesive way.

Second, learn multiple languages. For most historians, the areas they are interested in will require reading documents that are written in other languages. For example, if you are interested in ancient history, you should learn German, Greek, or French. You may want to study one of the dead languages like Sumerian, Latin, or Middle Egyptian. For prehistory, consider focusing on understanding hieroglyphs. Or focus on linguistics, which is the study of languages, how they develop, how they change over time, and the interconnection between languages.

Third, practice critical thinking. Critical thinking is the ability to quickly and accurately analyze and evaluate information that is gathered from what you see, what you read, and what you experience. It is the ability to understand your personal biases and remove them from your analysis. To become a critical thinker, join the debate

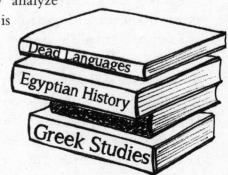

club, or discuss politics, religion, or legal cases with someone who has an opposing viewpoint from yours.

FRESH MEAT *profile*

MATTHEW J. BROUSSARD, NATIONAL ENDOWMENT FOR THE HUMANITIES SCHOLAR, 2011, 2013, 2014
IMPACT EARLY COLLEGE HIGH SCHOOL
BAYTOWN, TEXAS
AGE: 16

When did you first discover that you liked studying history?

I can't remember a time when I haven't been interested in history. As a preschooler, I was obsessed with dinosaurs. I remember being so excited as I ran up the sidewalk leading to the Houston Museum of Natural Science that I fell and skinned my knees. I just wanted to see those dinosaurs! Of course, my parents showed me the Egyptian mummies and artifacts, as well as all the other permanent exhibits, and I loved it.

What history competitions have you entered and what awards have you won?

All sixth graders in my school district are required to compete in the Kenneth E. Behring National History Day (NHD) Contest and submit a project based on that year's theme. Students are allowed to choose between an exhibit, a paper, a documentary, a website, or a performance category in which to compete. You may enter as an individual or in a group as large as five people.

As a sixth grader, I decided to do an individual performance because I had just finished performing as Chip in Disney's

Beauty and the Beast. That year, the theme was "Innovations in History: Impact and Change." I chose anesthesia as my topic and portrayed William T. G. Morton, the discoverer of anesthesia. I won the school, district, and state competitions, but placed third in my preliminary room, so I didn't advance to the finals.

In seventh grade, I portrayed Ben Franklin as he explained the intricate details behind the Treaty of Paris, 1783. I placed first in the nation. Dr. Gorn said, "You will forever be known as an NEH [National Endowment for the Humanities] Scholar!"

In eighth grade, I placed sixth in the nation as Thomas Jefferson. And in ninth grade, at the 2013 NHD competition, I placed first in the Senior Individual Performance category portraying John Hay, [President Abraham] Lincoln's secretary. I had never seen anyone win two years in a row, so I decided to quit while on top.

Then the 2014 competition began. I felt an irresistible force drawing me to compete again. I explored the origins of the Fourth Amendment and chose my dear friend Dr. [Benjamin] Franklin to tell the amazing story, once again.

More than half a million students compete in local history contests. What steps do you take to achieve a winning entry?
I look everywhere for information! The internet is my starting point. I go to historians and authors for advice. You would be surprised at how graciously top historians respond to a kid. Libraries, old newspaper databases, plantations, diaries, pictures, and historic sites are possibilities. The Library of Congress is always available.

I focus on solid research from every primary source I can lay my hands on. This means spending hours in the basement of Rice University, at their great research library. I search their catalog from home and go prepared to find my materials. It's about forty minutes from my home, so my parents drive me there early and we spend the entire day.

I always start in July—the previous competition ends in June. A lot of work gets done before my school year ever begins. I've learned that as I immerse myself in my research, my preconceived ideas are radically changed. I think about everything in light of whatever topic I'm studying. I suppose that extreme commitment to the project is what separates the winners from everyone else. I also think that my topic choices make a difference. The judges have to see that your project shows impact over time, that this event or person affected change.

What was your 2014 history topic and your experience at the competition?

While researching for a speech on the Fourth Amendment, I found the story of James Otis and the 1761 Writs of Assistance case. The more I looked into the case, the more I realized how perfect it would fit into the NHD theme. My speech received such a passionate response that people were suggesting I compete one more time. The speech evolved into a performance and took me even further back in history than I had anticipated.

By a rather serendipitous turn of events, the Magna Carta, for the first time in eight hundred years, journeyed from Hereford Cathedral in England and took up residence at the Houston Museum of Natural Science! My family visited this magnificent document in the most enchanting exhibit I have ever seen. I was able to get a guided tour by Rich Hutting, and I included the Magna Carta in my presentation.

I advanced to the national contest for the fifth time, never anticipating the blessings I would receive. A couple of weeks before the contest, Kim Fortney, Deputy Director of NHD, called and asked if I would present at a VIP reception at the Smithsonian Museum of American History for Kenneth E. Behring [the man for whom the contest is named]! Wow! I was overwhelmed and overjoyed beyond my wildest imagination.

The next day, I won the Magna Carta Prize, sponsored by the American Bar Association—a completely unexpected award—and first place in the nation once again.

How do you balance your schoolwork, outside activities, and your research for competitions?

I focus on time management! I'm also working on college classes and preparing for the role of Danny Zuko in *Grease*. I work ahead when I have extra time. I also use travel time to and from school to read. One thing's for sure: I am never bored!

Where do you see yourself in ten years?

As of now, I hope to be studying in England at either Oxford or Cambridge. After I received the Magna Carta Prize, Hereford Cathedral heard about it and asked the British Consulate to present some gifts to me, to commemorate my work. At that ceremony, they shared with me the possibility that I might apply for the Marshall Scholarship and experience an international education. I hope to realize that dream as I do my postgraduate work.

What is the most interesting thing you have discovered during your research?

The more I dig into a topic, the more I realize that things are never simple. There is always a complex series of events that could hinge on one thing happening or not happening. It always amazes me how interdependent we all are on one another and how things that happened centuries ago still affect us today, and how people who lived centuries ago took courageous steps, and sacrificed so much—for us!

Another thing that comes to mind is a particular essay by Dr. [Benjamin] Franklin. I learned that this famous statesman, philosopher, inventor, and scientist once wrote an essay titled "Fart Proudly." He posed the idea that research should be conducted in order to correct the public embarrassment of passing gas, perhaps by inducing a more pleasant aroma.

Genealogist

Genealogists study the history of families. They start with one person, living or dead, and then work their way backward in time, finding parents, grandparents, and great-grandparents. They dig into historical archives, searching for details of each person's life. Through careful research, they try to go back in time as far as possible.

To work as a professional genealogist, you don't need a college education, but taking a few classes will help with some of the skills you'll need to succeed. Since genealogists are usually self-employed, taking classes in business management, contract negotiations, time management, marketing, and sales would be a great place to start.

There are short, intense, weeklong courses offered at the Salt Lake Institute of Genealogy in Utah or Samford University's Institute of Genealogy and Historical Research in Alabama. If you're interested in working with federal records, consider taking the one-week course offered by the National Institute on Genealogical Research, which is held at the National Archives in Washington, DC.

Besides classes, you should join professional organizations to keep up-to-date with what is happening in the field. A good place to start is the Association of Professional Genealogists or the National Genealogical Society. Through these organizations, you will find opportunities to further your education by attending workshops and seminars.

Once you know that you want to become a genealogist, then you should apply for certification and accreditation. This can be done through the Board of Certification of Genealogists. There are six certifications:

- certified genealogist

- certified genealogical record specialist

- certified american lineage specialist

- certified american indian lineage specialist

- certified genealogical lecturer

- certified genealogical instructor

To further improve your chances of making a living as a genealogist, read magazines and journal articles written by genealogists. Explore local historical societies, libraries, archives, and historical sites. And, network with others in the field. Each time you talk to a fellow genealogist, librarian, or archivist, you will learn something new, find a solution to a problem, or discover new research techniques. Your local genealogical society is a great place to start gathering information and networking.

What Genealogists Work As

- Adoption specialists

- Archivists

- Editors

- Genealogy researchers

- Genetic specialists

- Heir searchers

- Historians

- Indexers

- Lineage specialists

- Photograph experts

- Web designers

- Writers

Layne G. Sawyer, MLS, CA
Manager of Reference Services, Oregon State
Archives
Salem, OR

When did you first become interested in history, historical data collection, and archiving, and decide to make it the focus of your career?

As a child, I was always interested in history and learning about the past. I loved to listen to my grandparents' stories about when they were kids and young adults. In high school, I excelled in the social sciences. So when I started college, I was leaning toward studying history and trying to find a career path that would work with this long-held interest. I earned my undergraduate degree in American history.

What education/work path did you take to get where you are today?

Because I always enjoyed studying history, I did well in those subjects in college. Trying to figure out a career that would allow me to pursue those interests led me to explore the idea of getting a degree in library science, and specifically from a program that offered a specialization in archives and manuscripts.

During my graduate studies, I did several internships at historical institutions, which allowed me to explore some of the different settings and duties that archivists performed. After completing my master of library science, I got my first professional job as a manuscripts curator at a state historical society. After several years in that position, I took a job at the state archives. That position involved more management duties and had me working exclusively with government or public records.

You are manager of references at the Oregon State Archives. What is held there, and what do you and your team do?

My position at the Oregon State Archives involves managing the reference unit, which is the unit that deals directly with the researchers who are using the archive's records to perform their research. The records we hold are all created by some level of government in Oregon. These types of records are generally referred to as *public records* and have specific laws that govern what must be preserved as permanent records and what type of access is provided.

Our records span the entire history of Oregon and include a few records that predate any type of organized government in the region, to records of the most recently completed legislative session. The reference archivists who work in my unit assist people trying to access specific information from those records. They also have knowledge of resources outside our holdings and can refer researchers to other sources for the information they are trying to find. I also manage the volunteers and student interns at our institution, represent the archives on a number of advisory groups, and participate in outreach activities that promote and publicize our program.

What jobs are available at the archives, and what skills and education do you require for your team members?

The professional positions at the archives require a college degree, with most employees having a graduate degree in history, library science, or a closely related field. In addition to the reference archivists, our staff includes records managers. They work with government agencies to help them manage the information and records they create, determine how long they need to be maintained, and identify the records that have historical value and need to be transferred to the archives for permanent preservation.

We also utilize volunteers and interns to assist staff in arranging and describing the records in the holdings. Student interns usually are college students who are interested in learning more about historical records and research, or exploring the archives as a possible career. We occasionally work with high school students who are interested in gaining work experience and are curious about what types of jobs might be available in the field.

Describe the Early Oregonians Project. Why is keeping a record of the lives of long-dead people important?
The archives developed the Early Oregonians database as a way of commemorating individuals who lived in Oregon prior to 1859, the year Oregon became a state. Oregon celebrated its sesquicentennial [150th anniversary] in 2009, and the database was also intended to be a legacy to future generations of residents.

Celebrating the history of the state at this significant milestone seemed like a good way to make people more aware of how the region developed and how white settlement impacted the area and the Native American inhabitants who had lived here for centuries, as well as how the new state impacted the history of the United States.

The database is used primarily by family history researchers who are looking for more information on ancestors who came to Oregon and the Pacific Northwest during that time period. There are also opportunities for these researchers to interact with our staff and share information they may have in family records that could help to create a more complete profile of an individual in the database.

What do you enjoy most about your work?
Although I personally perform more management functions, I always enjoy interacting with researchers and helping them to find the information that they need. Even in the instances where you might not be able to find the information they are searching for, it is a challenge to try to be creative and perhaps come up with clues or leads to other sources that might include some of the information they are looking for.

I think the most satisfying part of the job is when you can help somebody find information that they have been looking for and, in some cases, solve a long-standing family mystery.

What advice would you give a young person who is interested in working as an archivist or in genealogical research?
I would encourage them to seek out volunteer experiences in a historical institution. Most institutions are very welcoming to young people. You should be willing to devote a block of time on a regular basis and be very conscientious in your attendance. Be open to trying a variety of assignments, as most archives have numerous tasks that can be performed by volunteers willing to learn specific skills and perform them according to established standards.

How has the internet changed the business of archiving information? And what do you see as future trends in your field?
The growing amount of digital and electronic information has resulted in a dramatic change in the archival profession. Although digital information can be made accessible through the internet and other electronic means, it presents problems for archivists. The rapid changes in software and hardware are a hurdle that the profession must address to assure that

electronic or "born digital" information is not lost to future generations. The skills required of archivists also demand more knowledge in dealing with computers and the various types of digital information society now produces and expects to be able to retrieve when needed.

Discover your family history by charting a portion of your family tree. In this activity, you will document and research five generations of your family, starting with you. To keep track of the names, you'll make a genogram, which is also called a family tree.

MATERIALS
several sheets of white paper
pen or pencil
optional: photocopy machine

STEP ONE: PLANTING YOUR TREE
Your family tree begins with you! Take one sheet of paper and put your name at the bottom. Include your date of birth and the city and state where you were born. Beside your name, write the names, dates of birth, and places of birth for each of your brothers and sisters. All of you form the trunk of your family tree. Your future children will form the roots of the tree, but for now, let's focus on the people who came before you: the branches of your tree.

STEP TWO: ADDING YOUR BRANCHES

Just above your name, write the name of your mom to the right and your dad to the left. If your mother changed her name when she married your dad, use her maiden name—the last name she was given at birth. Just like you did in step one, record your parents' dates and places of birth. Draw a line between them and record the date they were married on that line.

Hint: Leave plenty of space between each person on your family tree. For example, don't put your parents too close together or it will be difficult to record their brothers and sisters (your aunts and uncles). Try to divide the paper evenly between names. As you gather more information, you may have to start over, creating a tree that has room for every name.

To the right of your mom, list her brothers and sisters, and their birth dates and places of birth. Do the same for your dad, putting his siblings to the left.

STEP THREE: CLIMBING HIGHER

Above your father's name, write the names of his parents (your paternal grandparents), with his mother on the right and his father on the left. Record their dates and places of birth, as well as the day they got married. Do the same thing with your mother's parents (your maternal grandparents).

Continue this chart until you have found your great-great-grandparents' information—your grandparents' grandparents. Your parents may know some of this information, but if possible, you may want to ask your grandparents for their help. Be sure to record the brothers and sisters of each person as you go higher on your tree.

A simple tree will look like this:

163

*great-grandmother's mom's
mom & dad*

*great-grandmother's mom's
mom & dad*

*great-grandmother's dad's
mom & dad*

*great-grandmother's dad's
mom & dad*

*great-grandfather's mom's
mom & dad*

*great-grandfather's mom's
mom & dad*

*great-grandfather's dad's
mom & dad*

*great-grandfather's dad's
mom & dad*

great-grandmother's mom & dad

great-grandmother's mom & dad

great-grandfather's mom & dad

great-grandfather's mom & dad

Grandmother's mom & dad

Grandmother's mom & dad

Grandfather's mom & dad

Grandfather's mom & dad

Grandmother & grandfather

Grandmother & grandfather

Mom   *Dad*

You — Your siblings

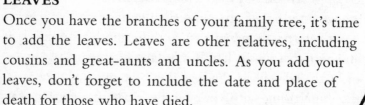

STEP FOUR: ADDING THE LEAVES

Once you have the branches of your family tree, it's time to add the leaves. Leaves are other relatives, including cousins and great-aunts and uncles. As you add your leaves, don't forget to include the date and place of death for those who have died.

8

Embracing the Dead in the Arts

Funerary Art

Any work of art that holds or is intended to hold human remains, or is a memorial to the dead, is called *funerary art*. Funerary art in the ancient past was intended to be used in the afterlife, define relationships, or soothe the spirits so they didn't bother the living. Today, it is used to remind the living of past events or in remembrance of an individual or individuals.

As you learned in chapter seven, there are thousands of monuments in the United States. On national, state, and local levels, there are men and women who work to create, erect, and maintain those monuments to the dead. Their jobs vary greatly, but are usually found within the NPS, state parks, monument manufacturing companies, and large cemeteries.

For most people, a small plaque adorns the spot where they are buried. Because cemeteries are trying to save space and keep maintenance costs down, the plaque usually lies flat to the ground, so it's easier to mow over it. With so little space, it is up to the family to choose wording and engravings that best suit their deceased loved one. For those who can afford it, and are allowed to by the cemetery, a unique monument is easily ordered, and the design is as limitless as their imaginations.

Famous Funerary Art

1. **The Judenplatz Holocaust Memorial** in Vienna, Austria. It was built in 2000 as a memorial to sixty-five thousand Austrian victims of the Holocaust, the organized killing of Jews ordered by German Chancellor Adolf Hitler.

2. **The Mausoleum at Halicarnassus** in Turkey. A tomb built around 350 BCE for Mausolus, who was a provincial governor, and his wife. It was designed by the Greek architects Satyros and Pythius of Priene. It stood about 148 feet (45 meters) tall and was considered one of the Seven Wonders of the Ancient World. Today, the site is in ruins.

3. **The Pyramids of Giza** near Cairo, Egypt. These pyramids are the tombs of Khufu, Khafre, and Menkaure, rulers of Egypt during the Fourth Dynasty, around 2500 BCE. They were built to protect the pharaohs' bodies and to last forever.

4. **The Taj Mahal** in Agra, Uttar Pradesh, India. The tomb of Mumtaz Mahal, the third wife of the Mughal Emperor Shah Jahan. It took sixteen years to build, from 1632 to 1648, and is considered an artistic masterpiece and the finest example of Mughal architecture.

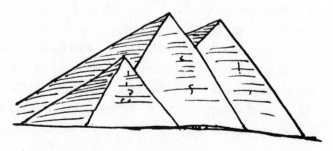

5. **The Terracotta Army at the Mausoleum of the First Qin Emperor** in Lintong District, Xi'an, Shaanxi province, China. Qin Shi Huang (260–210 BCE) was the first emperor of China. A terracotta army of over eight thousand men, 130 chariots, and 670 horses was placed in his tomb to protect him in the afterlife.

6. **The Vietnam Veterans Memorial** in Washington, DC. Completed in 1982, this gabbro rock memorial wall is 246 feet 9 inches (75.21 meters) long. Etched in it are the names of 58,272 men and women who were either killed in action or missing in action during the Vietnam War.

POLLY MORGAN, SCULPTOR
LONDON, ENGLAND

You are an artist and a taxidermist. When did you first become interested in taxidermy and decide to make it the focus of your artistic career?
When I had just turned twenty-four. I had tried out so many things, and this was the latest in a long line; only this one stuck.

What education/work path did you take to get where you are today, including what you did as a teenager, if relevant?
None of my education is especially relevant to my day-to-day work: GCSEs [General Certificate of Secondary Education tests taken when a student is between 15 and 17 years old. There are individual tests for every subject], A-Levels [General Certificate of Education Advanced Levels, tests given to students planning to go to college], acting classes, a college degree in English

literature, photography classes, and a journalism course. However, everything was relevant in that I ended up doing taxidermy via a process of elimination, so I feel it was all a process I needed to go through.

What process do you go through when beginning an art piece?

The idea usually comes first. I then collage it together on the computer using Photoshop. That's where I play around with the scale and elements until I'm happy with how it looks and I'm ready to start making the piece. Deciding on an idea good enough to undertake is the hardest part. The making of the piece is the most enjoyable.

You have created a lot of art pieces using birds. Why do you use them and what do you find so fascinating about them?

Their delicacy and fragility to start with. I also found that, as they can fly, there was a flexibility to their bodies I can exploit. I have since found this to be even more the case with snakes. Positioning birds "as dead" has more visual power since we aren't used to seeing them so still.

Your work is beautiful, but some of your pieces can make the viewer feel sad. How do you respond when someone thinks a piece is macabre or disrespectful of animals?

I think it's disappointing. To view my work as macabre is to be unable to get past the fact that my material comes from a dead animal. Charcoal drawings are made from burnt wood, but would never be considered intrinsically macabre. It is also to miss the point that my work is so often about the cycle of life and the triumph of life over death.

I find the notion of taxidermy disrespecting animals equally baffling. I think it is to foist human sentimentality onto them, when they arguably don't mourn their dead. They quite frequently eat them. I think the worst thing I can be accused of, by taking dead animals out of the food chain, is depriving the odd crow of a meal.

Where do you get the animals you use in your artwork?
From a wide variety of sources: vets, farmers, breeders, pet owners, and cat-kill. The longer I've been practicing taxidermy, the wider my network of sources has become. Once I know what I'm making and what animal I need, I look for people who are likely to be with that animal at the point of its death. I then approach them and ask if they're willing to contact me if and when the animal dies. I arrange to have it collected and brought to my studio.

What is the most exciting piece you've worked on, and why was it important to you?
I recently flew out to Bahrain to taxidermy a baby giraffe. Even though the final work was destined for Britain, I had to taxidermy it over there, as it wasn't possible to get the frozen body back into the country. I spent weeks arranging for a studio to be set up out there and took my assistant, Kim, with me. We finished the project in ten days. It's not the sort of thing I'll probably be offered again anytime soon. It was such a privilege to get to know, intimately, such a striking creature's anatomy.

What advice would you give a young person who is interested in becoming an artist?
Try to absorb as many influences as possible. If you get inspiration from too narrow a source, you will most likely become derivative [unoriginal]. It's paramount to find your own voice; people respond best to authenticity. You have to overcome your fear of failure and to make art and allow it to be seen. You will fail, most likely over and over again, but success doesn't just happen. And if it appears to, it is rarely sustainable.

Bodies: The Exhibition

Bodies: The Exhibition is a popular and controversial art and education exhibit. It has toured the world and been seen by over fifteen million people. The controversy comes from those who are concerned about the ethics of displaying dissected human bodies for others to view. In contrast, other people see the display as a beautiful work of art, or as an educational and informative way to understand the most beautiful machine ever created.

There are about two hundred bodies in the various exhibits, all donated for research by the Chinese government. The bodies were preserved through a process called *plastination*, which was discovered and patented by Gunther von Hagens in the 1970s. In this process, the inside of each cell is replaced with silicone rubber, polyester, or epoxy resin, making the body no longer at risk of decay. The bodies for this exhibit were preserved and dissected at Dalian University in Liaoning, China.

The first display is a skeleton. Then, as the visitor moves through the following displays, more layers are shown, like the nervous system, the circulatory system, and the digestive system. There are also exhibits that show how disease and tobacco use destroy the body.

PHOTOGRAPHER

In the early 1800s, cameras became popular, and photographers began to take pictures of the dead. Because it took over five minutes to capture an image, they were the ideal subjects. As the cost of getting a photograph decreased, many middle-class families took photographs of their dead as a last memory, sometimes even posing with them. Creepy!

Writer

Professional Obituary Writers

Professional obituary writers are skilled journalists, avid researchers, and compassionate people. They feel it is an honor and privilege to write the story of a person's life and carry out that mission with wit and skill. To work as a professional obituary writer, you need good writing and research skills, and probably a bachelor's degree in writing or journalism.

The obituaries of movie stars, business icons, and ordinary people are read each day by thousands of readers. There are even obituary fans who pore over whatever is written about someone who has died that day. A well-written obituary tells an interesting story, connects with readers, stirs emotions, and gives a sense of the deceased's personality and character.

Types of Obituary Writing

1. Newspaper obituaries, which are written by newspaper staff writers.

2. Death announcements, which are written and paid for by family members.

3. Obituaries, which are written by professional writers and paid for by family members. Professional writers are used by those who are preplanning their end-of-life arrangements, family members of the deceased who want professional help in honoring their loved one, and newspaper editors who want a feature story about someone who has died in their community.

Each obituary is a story of a life. It is a short biography that focuses on the person's achievements, work history, and contributions to society and family. Obituary journalists prepare biographical information and, if time allows, interview some of the people who knew the deceased. Once they have gathered what information they can find, they try to write an interesting and compelling article.

In large city newspapers, writing all the obituaries is a huge task. There are many obituaries for ordinary people and often one or more that require a lengthy biography. In small newspapers, where the idea of preserving history is still practiced, longer obituaries are common. They may include photographs, be written as a feature-length article, or even be printed on the front page.

Book Writer

Many people write books about the dead. From the discovery of a new civilization to current research on dying, nonfiction book writers are finding new and interesting ways to write about the dead. In fiction, the dead theme is everywhere, including in books for younger readers.

DEATH IN MIDDLE-GRADE AND TEEN FICTION

- *Going Home* by Jamie Lynn Yeager
- *Elsewhere* by Gabrielle Zevin
- *Song of the Pearl* by Ruth Nichols
- *Hachiko Waits* by Lesléa Newman
- *The Fault in Our Stars* by John Green
- *Ghostgirl* series by Tonya Hurley

Performing Artist

Playing Dead on TV or in the Movies

Playing dead on television or in the movies is not for sissies. It is hard work, long hours, and low pay, but with all the shows that use dead bodies, there's plenty of work. Fiction dramas like *NCIS*, *Law & Order*, and *Bones*, and documentary reenactments like those on *48 Hours* or *Countdown to Murder*, have dead people in each episode and are keeping actors like Chuck Lamb busy.

WORKING STIFF *profile*

CHUCK LAMB, ACTOR
COLUMBUS, OHIO

When did you first become interested in playing dead on television or in film and decide to make it the focus of your career?
It started as a funny conversation with my wife, Tonya, while we were watching a crime drama. I told her that I had always wanted to see my name in a movie or TV credits. Later that night, I had a dream that I was the dead body on a crime drama show. I woke Tonya up and explained to her that anybody can just lie around and almost every show needs a dead body. I don't even have to know how to act, and with my pale looks and features, maybe? And I've lain still for *years*, like a coach potato, watching TV, with a bowl of snacks balanced on my tummy. I'm a natural!

What education/work path did you take to get where you are today?

I have always wanted to make people laugh, and I was the class clown in school and at work. I think we should laugh more and be happy. When I was young, I put the whole acting thing on hold because I had to work to support my children.

You started out as an information technology manager. Why did you decide to leave that job and pursue a career in acting?

It didn't actually happen quite like that. We didn't know that the website and the media would root so much for me! It started as a joke, and then a website my wife and I made for laughs. It was our dream to be on just *one* TV show or movie. Then the website exploded with over fifty million hits and has been seen in 155 countries!

What is a day like on the set for a person playing a dead character?

Long! A day will actually start at 6:00 AM. There is a lot, and I do mean *a lot*, of waiting. If you think you are going to waltz in, get makeup, take your shot, and dance away, you are dead wrong.

You must remember that your scene is one of many that will be shot that day, and the major-name stars do not like waiting around for an extra to be shot in a dead scene. There's a pecking order and protocol that is used on set. If you are an extra in a show, then you are not allowed to speak with the stars unless they speak first. No pictures, no autographs, nothing. You have your area to be in and they have their private area. I've been lucky enough to have my own trailer a couple of times. If a bigger-name star sees you have a trailer, they will usually come around and ask who you are.

What do you enjoy most about your work?
The traveling, meeting new people, and the chance to get to meet some of my idols from TV and motion pictures I saw while I was growing up. I have had the pleasure of meeting Debbie Reynolds, Mickey Rooney, and many other stars while attending red carpet and autograph events. We got to go the Oscars in 2006, and it was one of the greatest nights of my life.

Can you tell us about your favorite job?
Yes. I was asked to appear at the Fangoria horror convention for three days in Hollywood. I was surrounded by zombies, killers, ghosts, wrestlers, and stars of some of my favorite movies of all time. I was like a kid, in awe of being part of something like that. If you ever get a chance to attend a convention event, make sure to go. Everyone has fun.

What advice would you give a young person who is interested in working as an actor?
Don't be just the next person in line. Set yourself apart from everyone else in the room somehow . . . whether it be your humor, good attitude, or something you say that the casting director will remember—even if it's just a great attitude.

Never quit living your dream. Try to think outside the box to set yourself apart from everyone else. Do you know how many beautiful male models would like to get the publicity I get? But all of those handsome guys all look alike to me, ha ha ha. Dare to be different!

Can you offer some tips for success to students planning to pursue a career in acting?
The most important thing I would say is make sure you stay in school. Casting directors and producers do not want to hire

someone who can't understand their instructions. You never know what useful information you may pick up in school that will help you out later in life.

Immerse yourself in the role, even if it's just playing dead. I started out playing dead, but now, many times, I get to speak lines and actually do some acting. Hey, did you know Kevin Costner played a dead guy in one of his first movies, *The Big Chill*?

Looking Dead *activity*

MATERIALS
plastic bugs
nontoxic glue that works on skin
liquid or cake foundation makeup in a color that is several
   shades lighter than your natural skin tone
makeup application sponges
bowl
baby powder
blue powdered eye shadow
large makeup brush
red eyeliner
brown powdered eye shadow
blue-gray lipstick or eye shadow pencil
clear nail polish
yellow food coloring
fake blood

DIRECTIONS

1. Wash your face and any other skin you want exposed, like hands and feet. Use warm, soapy water. Rinse thoroughly and pat dry. This will remove the oil from your skin and help the makeup stay on longer. Note: if you want to add insects to your face, do it here, before applying makeup.

2. Using a makeup sponge, apply the liquid foundation evenly over the clean skin.

3. In a small bowl, thoroughly mix baby powder with a small amount of blue eye shadow. Start with about a ten to one ratio, but this can vary greatly depending on how dark your blue eye shadow is. The mixture should end up a very light gray. If you want to look like a cold corpse, add a touch more blue.

4. Using a large makeup brush, spread the gray powder evenly over your skin.

5. Using the makeup brush, apply blue eye shadow to your eyelids and under your eyes. Remember that less is best. You can always add more if you need to.

6. Using the red eyeliner, carefully draw a light red line beneath your upper eyelashes and above your lower lashes.

7. Mix brown eye shadow with a bit of baby powder. Using the makeup brush, fill in the contours under your cheekbones, between your fingers, and anywhere you want a bit of contrast to give the skin a sunken look.

8. Fill in your lip color using blue-gray lipstick or a similar-colored eye shadow pencil.

9. Mix a few drops of yellow food coloring into the clear fingernail polish bottle. Paint your nails.

10. Add fake blood to look like it is draining from the corner of your mouth, from your ears, or from a wound that's hidden under your hair.

When your makeup is done, mess up your hair, put on some tattered and torn clothing, and practice your cold, dead, unblinking stare.

Playing Dead as a Tour Guide

In cities and cemeteries around the world, entertainers pretend to be the living dead. They guide their guests through dark streets, telling stories of murder and mayhem, or through creepy cemeteries filled with ghosts, goblins, and the undead. These tours are popular events for those who like a scary time. For some tours, becoming a tour guide requires that you be over eighteen years old and a high school graduate. For others, especially national battlefields, you'll need to become a licensed guide and know a lot about the history of the area.

FIVE GHOSTLY DESTINATIONS

The Catacombs in Paris, France. There are tours of a vast underground network of tunnels, deep beneath the city, where the remains of over six million dead Parisians are interred. It is a top destination for ghost hunters.

- 🜂 **The Ghosts of Gettysburg Tours.** Tours of the town of Gettysburg and the battlefields where about fifty-one thousand men were wounded or killed in a three-day skirmish during the Civil War. Some of the soldiers died immediately, and some endured weeks of suffering before they died. Many say that their spirits remain and the area is haunted by these dead soldiers.

- 🜂 **Savannah, Georgia.** Ghost tours in this city are popular because parts of the city are built on top of thousands of graves. It is said that the city is teeming with paranormal activity.

- 🜂 **London, England.** Ghost tours in London are extremely popular. In the dark and foggy streets, tour guides have tales from across the centuries of ghosts and murderers—stories of Bloody Mary, Jack the Ripper, and the ghosts of people who lived during the black plague.

- 🜂 **Salem, Massachusetts.** Salem is a city filled with ghosts. From the witch trials of the late 1600s to the lost souls who haunt the Turner-Ingersoll Mansion (the House of the Seven Gables), this town is filled with lively tours and ghostly adventures.

Professional Mourner

In some countries, people are paid to attend funerals and grieve for the dead. Paid mourners are a tradition that began in the Middle East and China, dating back to Old Testament times. In these cultures, a lack of tears at a funeral is a dishonor to the dead and a disgrace for the family. For many, this problem is solved by paying professionals to attend the funeral. They are expected to weep and wail and get the other mourners to join with them.

Professional mourners are also hired to fill in for relatives who are too busy to attend.

In England, paid mourners are briefed about the deceased's life and given a role to play: the friend, a coworker, a golfing buddy, and so forth. At the funeral, they are expected to mingle, offer condolences, and look appropriately sad. In typical English style, they are not expected to weep or wail, but remain stoic and dignified, possibly shedding a single token tear. In the United States, the job of professional mourner is limited. There are a few funeral homes that hire them for special funerals. Planning this as a career is probably not a good idea.

Celebrating the Dead

In many countries, there are special days when the people celebrate and remember their dead.

- ♀ **All Saint's Day** is a national holiday in traditionally Catholic countries such as Portugal. It takes place on November 1 and is a time to remember the dead saints and the unknown martyrs of the faith.

- ♀ **Dia de los Muertos** (Day of the Dead) is a holiday that began in Mexico and is now celebrated throughout Latin America and anywhere there is a large Hispanic community. On November 1 and 2, communities hold festivals and celebrations to honor the dead. Families clean the graves of loved ones and construct small altars. Children enjoy eating skulls made from sugar and other candies shaped like skeletons.

- ♀ **Famadihana** (the Turning of the Bones) is a celebration unique to the island of Madagascar. During the winter months, the bodies of ancestors are removed from their tomb and rewrapped in clean cloths. The family members then raise them above their heads and dance with the corpses as a way of letting go of their grief and celebrating their dead loved one. Depending on the family, this ceremony takes place every two to seven years.

- **Halloween** (or All Hallows' Eve) is celebrated on October 31 in many western countries like the United States and Canada. It originally marked the beginning of a three-day period of remembering the dead, especially saints and martyrs for the Christian faith. Today, it is a night set aside for parties, carving pumpkins into jack-o'-lanterns, visiting haunted houses, watching horror films, and letting kids wear costumes and go trick-or-treating.

- **The Hungry Ghost Festival** is celebrated in China during the seventh lunar month, in July or August. Restless spirits are thought to roam the earth, and on the fifteenth night, food is offered to them and any dead ancestors who are visiting at the time. During the festival, devotees make offerings to the gods of the underworld in hopes of gaining luck.

- **Lemuralia** was celebrated by the ancient Romans as a way of banishing harmful spirits from a house. On this day, the head of the household woke at midnight, washed his hands three times, and walked through the house throwing black beans over his shoulder while repeating a chant. The three-day event also included festivals and games.

- **Obon Festival** is a five-hundred-year-old Buddhist celebration, observed mainly in Japan. During the festival months of July and August, ancestor spirits return to visit their relatives. Obon is often marked by family reunions, and lanterns are lit to guide the spirits to and from the other world.

♀ **Pitru Paksha** is a sixteen-day Hindu festival that is celebrated in September. People offer food to their ancestors and make donations to charity as a way of honoring the people who have impacted their lives. Traditionally, it is believed that the ancestors come to visit and bless their family during this time.

♀ **Qingming Festival** is celebrated in China at the beginning of April. It is a day set aside for sweeping and clearing away debris from tombs. With cremation becoming more popular, today the festival includes praying and offering flowers and fake paper money to the dead.

9

Putting the Dead to Work

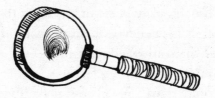

Sometimes, the remains of the dead are not buried or preserved, but put to work for other purposes. There are interesting jobs in a variety of fields, from using human bodies for medical education to making furniture from dead trees.

Putting Human Remains to Work

In order for a human body to be used for any purpose, it must be donated by written consent of the person before death or by the next of kin after death. From ancient times to today, there have been unwritten and written rules about the rights of the dead. Their foremost rights are to not be physically abused, and to be treated with dignity, buried properly, and left in peace. There are laws in every state that try to protect these rights and adhere to the Uniform Anatomical Gift Act which lays out who can donate a body and how the body must be treated. Even when a body is donated willingly, the expectation is that it will be treated with dignity and, when the research is done, buried or cremated and left in peace.

Donated Bodies

Bodies of dead humans are only used for education or research. Any time a body or a part of a body is sold for profit, a crime has been committed. For education, they are used in medical schools to teach anatomy to medical students and surgery to surgical residents. Almost any surgery can be practiced on a cadaver, and it is important for surgeons to have this kind of training before performing surgery on a living person.

For research, usually only parts of the body are used. Researchers use blood, tissue, or organs to further their knowledge of diseases like cancer or viral and bacterial infections, and  to further their understanding of how cells divide or how cells react to various treatments.

Jobs in this area include those within a company that handles body donations, jobs in the morgue of the institution where the body is sent, professors who teach medical school students, and the many researchers within various medical specialties. The medical school students who learn anatomy by studying the body are not paid, but they are on the path to a well-paid career in medicine.

BODY FARMS

Body farms are open-air crime labs where bodies, sometimes as many as fifty, are studied as they decompose. At the Freeman Ranch in Texas, a twenty-six-acre outdoor human decomposition laboratory—the largest in the world—scientists study the rate of decay, the patterns of decay, and the overall process of decay under a myriad of conditions. The results of their research are used by forensic scientists and law enforcement.

Henrietta Lacks: First Human Cell Line Used for Medical Research

Henrietta Lacks was born in 1920 in Roanoke, Virginia. When she was four years old, her mother died, and she went to live with her grandfather. In 1941, at the age of twenty-one, she married David Lacks, and the couple moved to Baltimore, Maryland.

Four months after her youngest child was born, Henrietta went to Johns Hopkins University hospital, the only hospital in the area that took black patients. She complained of pain in her abdomen and was diagnosed with cancer. During her treatment, doctors removed a section of healthy tissue and a section of diseased tissue. She received what treatment was available at the time, but on October 4, 1951, she died at the age of thirty-one.

Interestingly, Henrietta's story doesn't end there. The tissue that was removed from her body was sent to Dr. George Otto Gey at the Tissue Culture Laboratory at Johns Hopkins University. He soon realized that her cancer cells were unique. They could easily be kept alive and reproduced. He could take one cell, multiply it, and grow an entire cell line. Gey named the sample "HeLa" after Henrietta.

The cell lines from Henrietta are considered immortal, since they don't die after dividing one or two times. Henrietta's HeLa cells were used to develop a polio vaccine and were the first successfully cloned human cells. Since then, the HeLa cells have continued to multiply. Scientists have produced over twenty tons of her cells! They were used in research that led to almost eleven thousand patents and over seventy thousand medical studies.

BOOKS BOUND IN HUMAN SKIN

Binding a book in human skin, called *anthropodermic bibliopegy*, may seem strange today, but in the past, it was more common. There is evidence of books wrapped in skin dating back to the sixteenth century. Often this was used as a way to memorialize a family member.

In 2014, experts at Harvard University learned that a volume in their collection was bound using human skin. The book, *Des destinees de l'ame*, was written by French writer Arsène Houssaye. It was given as a gift to Dr. Ludovic Bouland, who then bound it in the skin of a mental patient who died of a stroke. A note in the book, written by Bouland, said, "A book about the human soul deserved to have a human covering." The book was given to Harvard in 1934 by a book collector.

Donated Organs and Tissue

Much like donating an entire body, anyone can choose to donate specific organs or tissue. These donations can only be used for transplant into another person or for research. Commonly transplanted organs include the kidney, pancreas, liver, heart, lung, and intestine. Other donated body parts include skin, bone, or heart valves. According to the United Network for Organ Sharing, in 2013 almost twenty-nine thousand organs and countless numbers of other parts were donated.

Human organs, tissue, and cells from the deceased are used in laboratories across the country for research. Whether the donation is healthy or diseased, researchers can use stem cells, bone marrow, islet cells, tumor tissue, cell lines, and DNA. They also use donations from donors with rare diseases and the human immunodeficiency virus (HIV). Research is done at the National Institutes of Health, universities, drug companies, and biotechnology companies. To work on any type of research using human organs, tissues, or cells, you need to have a doctorate or be under the supervision of someone with a doctorate.

Jobs in this area include those within the companies that register and document donations, those that transport patients to transplant hospitals or deliver organs to transplant hospitals, the hospitals where the transplants take place, and the doctors who perform the surgeries.

WORKING STIFF profile

SUSAN ORLOFF, CHIEF SURGEON, DIVISION OF ABDOMINAL ORGAN TRANSPLANTATION
SURGICAL DIRECTOR, LIVER TRANSPLANTATION, OREGON HEALTH AND SCIENCE UNIVERSITY
PORTLAND, OREGON

When did you first become interested in medicine and decide to make it the focus of your career?
I originally applied to the University of California Davis School of Veterinary Medicine and was accepted on the condition I first work for a veterinarian for a year. So I went to work at an emergency animal clinic. The main focus of my job was to euthanize animals, including cats and dogs that were hit by cars. Many of them could have been saved but, unfortunately, no one

had insurance for these animals. This led me to an epiphany. I would continue to love and care for animals as a hobby, but not care for them medically as a profession. Instead of becoming a veterinarian, I decided I'd rather take care of human beings whose lives could be helped and potentially saved.

What education/work path did you take to get where you are today?

I attended the University of California San Diego and graduated with a BS in biology. I chose not to go the pre-med or pre-vet route. However, I did strive for excellence. I studied hard, learned the material, and was able to achieve excellent grades. Based on those grades and my Graduate Records Examination (GRE) and Medical College Admission Test (MCAT) scores, I had the choice whether to attend a veterinary or a medical school. The bottom line is that it's not about being smart. It's about having passion and dedication for what you do and finding motivation in knowing how your work can impact the future.

How did you decide that becoming a surgeon and then a transplant surgeon were the right career choices for you?

I started out in internal medicine in 1984, during the AIDS era when there were few treatments for the disease. Patients were dying of AIDS-related complications, and I felt useless and helpless. I had just lost a patient to AIDS who was a very intelligent young man. I wandered by an operating room and heard rock and roll music as the surgeon was removing the appendix from another young man. I remember thinking, *They are making that young man better!* A switch went on in my head. I knew then that I wanted to become a surgeon—join a field where I could truly help people using my brain and my hands. And the rest is history.

[*In 1993, Dr. Orloff was in a biking accident and fractured her back and neck in six places. Her surgeon told her that her career as a surgeon was over. She would never be able to stand at an operating table for any length of time. She refused to accept that prognosis. With grit and determination, she retaught her body to work, starting with holding her head up and ending with regaining the fine motor skills in her hands and fingers.*]

I became a surgeon and specialized in the transplantation of organs. It is a uniquely magical field, especially when you realize how the grief over the death of a loved one can be eased through the gift of giving his or her organs to save the lives of others. When you think about that process, that circle of life, you can begin to appreciate what an incredible field transplantation is.

Your transplant work focuses on the liver. Why did you choose to become an expert in transplanting that organ?
In my mind, the liver is the most astonishing organ. Not only is it life sustaining, but it is the machinery of blood clotting, nutrition and protein, and carbohydrate metabolism. If it works properly, it allows an individual to live a great life. Additionally, the liver has a secret key: it can regenerate itself! This is remarkable!

As a transplant surgeon, you use organs that are taken from the dead in order to save lives. What are your thoughts on organ donation?
Every single individual should be an organ donor. The best thing that can come out of death is giving life to someone else, and now that possibility exists with transplantation.

As a woman who started her career in a very male-dominated field, what might a young woman face today should she decide to become a surgeon?
I never thought of myself as a "woman surgeon," only a surgeon. If you excel, you excel. It doesn't matter your gender.

Don't pay attention to any form of discrimination—it only takes away from what is important.

In medicine, we are all on the front lines. We must eliminate any and all persecution regarding race and gender. The bottom line is the patient's well-being. Those doctors who focus on anything else should find another career.

What advice would you give a young person who is interested in becoming a transplant surgeon?
Becoming a transplant surgeon is a career for someone who loves to work, pursue science, and values the ability to make life-changing decisions and perform life-extending operations. I believe that every career requires sacrifice and compromise—I choose to focus on how privileged I am to be able to work at the highest level of my talent and ability in a field that saves lives, helping patients when they most need it. If you want it, go for it. The sky's the limit.

HUMAN CRASH TEST DUMMIES

Before there were robotic crash test dummies, human cadavers were used to figure out how a car crash impacts the human body. Today, car manufacturers use dummies, but universities around the world still use human bodies to test a variety of impact scenarios. They use them because they give the most accurate data. These tests are funded by the National Highway Traffic Safety Administration and the Insurance Institute for Highway Safety. After the tests are complete, the data is shared with the automotive industry.

Putting Animal Remains to Work

Since the beginning of human existence, we have used animal skins for warmth, clothing, and housing. Whether it's a bearskin rug, a leather jacket, or a buffalo-skin tepee, animal skins are put to work for the benefit of people. Today, there are a lot of people who decry this practice. However, it is a reality in our lives, and the hope is that, throughout the process, each animal will be treated with some degree of respect. Most of the jobs in this field do not require a college education.

Tanner

A tanner is a person who *tans* skins, treats the skin of animals to be used for leather. Although tanning a deerskin can be done at home, most leather is made by large companies. About twenty companies make all the leather in the United States. Leather is used in many products, from couches and car seats to belts and purses. It is made by curing, shaving, treating, and finishing the hides of animals like sheep, deer, cows, and horses to create different kinds of leather called sheepskin, deerskin/buckskin, cowhide, and horsehide.

Slaughterhouse Worker

A slaughterhouse worker removes the hides from animals and cures them with salt to prevent decay. The hides are tied into bundles and shipped to tanneries.

Butcher

A butcher takes the carcass of an animal and prepares it for people or other animals to eat. Butchers work in grocery stores or special meat shops like fish markets or butcher shops, or they own their own businesses.

Upholsterer

Upholsterers work with leather to cover furniture or other seats, like those in cars, buses, or airplanes. An upholsterer must know how to shape foam, read and interpret patterns, create new patterns, and sew. Some upholsterers work for museums or restoration companies, repairing damaged leather on antiques and historic artifacts.

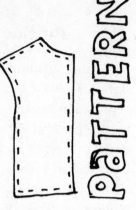

Fossil Fuels: Using Three-Hundred-Million-Year-Old Dead Animals and Plants

Fossil fuels were formed millions and millions of years ago, when the earth was covered in swampy land filled with trees and large, leafy plants. When the plants died, they formed layers of spongy material called *peat*. As the years passed, the peat was covered over by a layer called sedimentary rock. As the rock grew heavier, it pressed down on the peat, forced out all the water, and turned it into the three fossil fuels we use today: coal, oil, and natural gas. Fossil fuels provide 82 percent of the energy we use in the United States each year.

Besides gasoline for our cars and natural gas to heat our homes, fossil fuels are used to make the plastic we use every day. They are also used to make synthetic fibers, like nylon, polyester, and acrylic. And they are used in medicines, cosmetics, and lubricants.

Limestone: Using Millions-of-Years-Old Dead Ocean Animals

Limestone is a sedimentary rock that is formed when ocean animals die and their bones and shells sink to the ocean floor. These bones and shells contain calcium carbonate. Over millions of years, the weight of the ocean water crushes the remains and the pressure forms them into rocks. Many fossils are found within limestone.

Man has used limestone for thousands of years. The Egyptians used it to build their pyramids, and the early Romans mixed it with ash to make concrete and build their monuments and roads. Because it is a soft stone, it is easily carved. It was used on the Empire State Building in New York City and the United States Holocaust Memorial in Washington, DC.

Limestone is also used to refine sugar, make glass, and tan leather. It is used in the manufacture of iron and steel, and it is used to treat sewage and filter drinking water. Farmers use crushed limestone as part of the fertilizer they spread over their fields.

Dead Viruses and Vaccines

There are several ways that scientists make vaccines to fight diseases caused by viruses or bacteria. One way is to create an *inactivated* vaccine. To do this, they kill the disease-causing microbes using chemicals, heat, or radiation. Then they set the dead microbes to work.

The dead microbes are made into a vaccine, which is injected into a person. The dead microbes stimulate the immune system. The immune system believes there is a threat to the body and creates antibodies to fight it off. If or when the immune system comes in contact with the live virus or bacteria in the future, it's ready and able to create more antibodies and destroy the microbes before they can cause harm.

There are inactivated viral vaccines for polio, influenza, hepatitis A, and rabies. There are inactivated bacterial vaccines for typhoid, cholera, plague, and pertussis.

What's great about inactivated vaccines is that dead microbes can't reproduce and change, so they are safer to use, and they are easy to transport around the world in freeze-dried form. What's not so great is that they activate a weaker immune response than live-microbe vaccines. Thus, one or more booster shots are needed to maintain immunity.

FRESH MEAT
profile

JARED NATHAN, STUDENT RESEARCHER
LINCOLN K-8 CHOICE SCHOOL
ROCHESTER, MINNESOTA
AGE: 13

The program that Jared works with is called Integrated Science Education Outreach (InSciEd Out). It is a collaboration between the Mayo Clinic, Winona State University, and Rochester Public Schools. The program's goal is to introduce students to the wonderful world of scientific research by forming "a collaborative partnership committed to rebuilding K–12 science education curricula for the twenty-first century."

When did you first discover that you wanted to conduct research?

I was introduced to the InSciEd Out zebrafish curriculum at my school in second grade and found it very interesting. Since this idea of a more hands-on, engaging approach to science was available, I took to it eagerly.

In fifth grade, I had the opportunity to work with the zebrafish more and do more serious zebrafish experiments. I was able to present my fifth-grade work at an international zebrafish conference, and it was published in a zebrafish journal.

In seventh grade, I did a science project involving zebrafish embryos, and I took it to the state science fair. I also presented this project at an international zebrafish conference. I think that the fifth-grade project where I learned how to handle the fish and experiment with them, their habitat, and their breeding patterns was when I really got interested in science research, but the science fair project allowed me to expand on it.

What is it like to work in a laboratory?
Once you gather your materials in the lab, you can conduct your whole experiment there. Everything is available to you, even computers. And everything can be used by the students. In the lab at Lincoln, I mostly set up zebrafish experiments (e.g., counting and sorting fish and embryos, and preparing solutions) and observe them under the microscopes available while the experiment is in progress.

Where do the ideas for your research come from?
Sometimes current events or new products and innovations that come out inspire my research. Other times, it is school subjects or discussions, or a simple scientific process that sparks my interest. For example, my seventh-grade project was based on the effects of e-cigarettes, a controversial device that was gaining popularity among young people. I had heard about them and I was interested about the lack of regulations regarding them due to uncertainty about the harmful effects they could have.

If you could conduct research on anything you wanted to, what would you work on?
I would do an in-depth study on the chemical origins of mental illness in the brain, the effects of mental illness (specifically depression) on brain function (learning, control), and unconventional ways to treat the illnesses.

How do you balance your schoolwork and your extracurricular activities with your research?
I balance my schoolwork and extracurricular activities with my research by doing most of my experimentation in school,

where I know I can make up the classwork. In regards to homework, I balance homework and research by leaving time after school to work on presentations and research, treating the science equally to other schoolwork.

Where do you see yourself in ten years?
In ten years, I see myself finishing college and looking for a job in an undetermined field. Some things I'm interested in are engineering, writing, marine biology, and architecture.

Trees: The Ultimate Working Dead Plant

Trees are nature's most abundant and versatile renewable resource. When one is cut down, it dies. To replace it, a seed must grow or a seedling must be planted. Growing a new tree can take many, many years. To sustain this resource for future generations, scientists, conservationists, and the lumber industry must work together. They must develop a plan that will allow some trees to be harvested, require some areas to be replanted, and maintain forests which are the natural habitat for many plants, animals, and birds.

There are many jobs in the timber industry that don't require a college education. However, students who choose to major in wood and paper science become the designers and producers of many products that are made from wood. Here are a few of the degree programs you might use in the timber industry:

- energy specialist

- packaging engineer

- pulp and paper specialist

- resin technologist

- wood fiber acquisition and sales

- wood science and engineering

- wood technologist

If you'd rather not go to college, here are a few jobs that don't require a college degree.

Lumberjacks, or woodcutters, cut down trees using chain saws, harvesters, and feller bunchers. The tree's limbs are removed, and the logs are cut into lengths suitable for hauling to the sawmill. Today, huge machines do a lot of the work, but the job of lumberjack is still ranked one of America's worst jobs because of the danger, low pay, and unstable work.

Sawmill workers handle the logs that come in on trucks or on railcars. Log scalers measure the logs and sort them into species, size, and quality, which helps determine the selling price of the log. Some logs are then fed into the mill, where they are cut into dimensional lumber.

Log or lumber truck drivers drive semitrucks loaded with logs from the forest to the mill, or the cut lumber from the mill to the store, where it will be sold. A special driver's license is required to drive a semitruck.

Carpenters build the main framework of buildings, frame in walls, windows, and doorways, and sometimes install cabinets. Entry-level work is as an apprentice or on-the-job training.

Woodworkers make cabinets and furniture. Most work for companies, but some are self-employed craftsmen who make each item by hand. To become a skilled woodworker will take a minimum of three years of on-the-job training. Computer-controlled machinery is becoming more common.

10

Research, Extinction, and Other Dead Things

Not all careers working with the dead fall into the categories mentioned in the previous chapters. In this final chapter, you'll learn about jobs that focus on researching the dead, combating extinction, communicating with the dead, and working with a few other interesting dead things.

Researching the Dead

Anatomist

Anatomists study the structure of living things, often by dissecting dead things. Anatomists can be botanists who study the structure of plants down to the cellular level. They can be zoologists and veterinarians who study the structure of animals, or doctors who study the structures of the human body. Some anatomists focus their study on cells and try to find new and better ways to study them.

- Colleges and universities

- Government agencies

- Hospitals and clinics

- Medical schools

- Pharmaceutical companies

- Private research institutions

To work as an anatomist, you need a bachelor's degree in anatomy, biology, or botany to get an entry-level position as a research assistant or laboratory assistant. To advance in this career, you'll need a master's degree for some positions and a doctorate if you want to conduct research and teach at a university. In order to keep up in this continuously changing field of study, plan to take continuing education classes throughout your career.

Thanatologist

Thanatology is the scientific study of death. There are many disciplines related to this field. If you are interested in the process of dying or what happens immediately after death, consider one of these areas of study:

- **Artists, authors, and poets** study death as it relates to a culture or an individual, focusing on the emotional impact of death. Musicians study how music helps the dying meditate, relieves their anxiety, and lessens their pain.

- **Cultural anthropologists** study how present cultures and communities deal with death.

- **Cultural archaeologists** study how past cultures and communities dealt with death.

- **Forensic scientists** study the biology of death, what happens to the body as it dies and immediately afterward.

- **Medical ethicists** study the ethics around the dying. They try to answer questions like: Is it okay to allow someone to become addicted to a drug as they are dying? When is it okay to assist a person in ending his or her life? At what point should expensive medical treatments be stopped?

- **Psychiatrists** study how certain drugs aid or hinder how an individual copes with death.

- **Psychologists** study death as it relates to individuals and their family members. They focus on studying the fear of dying, the grieving process, and the process of accepting one's own death.

- **Sociologists** study how a society handles death.

MELANIE L. D. GREEN, MSc/PhD, FORENSIC SPECIALIST/
BIOLOGY REPORTING SCIENTIST
ROYAL CANADIAN MOUNTED POLICE (RCMP), NATIONAL
CENTER FOR FORENSIC SERVICES
EDMONTON, ALBERTA, CANADA

When did you first become interested in forensic genetic research and decide to make it the focus of your career?

I have always been interested in science and always loved mysteries. For my sixth birthday, I asked my parents for a microscope. I thought it was the best gift ever! I read all of the Nancy Drew and Hardy Boys books, and I tried not to miss a single episode of the television show *Murder, She Wrote*. It seemed natural that I would eventually become involved in using science to try to solve mysteries, either those of the human body or those of a criminal nature.

What education/work path did you take to get where you are today?

When I started university, I intended to become a physician, so I enrolled as a cell biology/microbiology and biochemistry major with a minor in chemistry. However, as I progressed from introductory to more advanced science courses, I realized that I loved working in a laboratory and considered becoming a biology researcher instead.

I was (and still am) fascinated by autoimmune diseases, that is, diseases where the body's immune system attacks itself. My MS and PhD projects focused on the autoimmune disease multiple sclerosis. It was during my PhD studies that I met a student who was leaving academia to pursue a career with the RCMP at the forensic laboratory in Ottawa, Ontario.

While I had always thought that being a forensic scientist would be an excellent and interesting job, I hadn't seriously considered it as a career choice. After several conversations with her about her new position, I decided forensic science was to be the focus of my career.

After being employed by the RCMP, I began an understudy training program to become a qualified forensic specialist/biology reporting scientist. This training program took approximately one year to complete and included extensive literature reviews and practical exercises in the identification of human biological materials, including blood, saliva, urine, hair, and feces, and in the analysis, interpretation, and comparison of DNA typing profiles. The training program also included job shadowing, court observation, written examinations, written and practical assignments, and mock trials.

Forensic genetic research sounds very interesting. Can you explain what you do?

When an exhibit comes into the laboratory, it is first examined and tested for biological materials including hair, blood, and other body fluids. If an area of interest is found, it is removed from the exhibit and forwarded for DNA analysis. The results of this DNA analysis are in an electronic format. My job is to use computer software to turn this electronic data into a DNA typing profile.

I then analyze and compare all the DNA typing profiles within a single case. If there are matching DNA typing profiles in the file, I perform statistical calculations (with the aid of another computer program) to estimate how rare or common those particular DNA typing profiles are within a particular population. Once I've finished all of the analyses, I write a report.

My other duties include testifying in court as an expert witness and giving presentations about forensic science and my work to students, laypeople, and law enforcement personnel.

I have worked on sexual assault, murder/manslaughter, burglary, and robbery cases.

What advice would you give a young person who is interested in becoming a forensic genetic researcher?

Talk to researchers at your university/college, talk to their students, and see what appeals to you. If possible, volunteer in some of the laboratories to gain a greater understanding of the type of work they are doing and the procedures and techniques being used in that laboratory.

Reading about it on the web is one thing, but getting your hands into it is quite another.

What do you see as future trends in forensic genetic research?
The future trends in forensic DNA analysis are always concerned with providing faster results. There are many companies working on systems that will allow the development of DNA typing profiles within minutes rather than hours.

STUDYING THE DEAD THROUGH STATISTICS

When a person dies, many health-related statistics are collected about the death. These statistics are reported to government agencies in every state, several major cities, and five US territories. From there, the information is sent to the Centers for Disease Control's National Center for Health Statistics (NCHS).

Within the NCHS, the National Vital Statistics System compiles the data so it can be used to see health problems and death trends throughout the nation. For example, they compile data about infant death in relation to the infants' geographic location, their parents' health, and the age at which they died.

The National Violent Death Reporting System accumulates data from eighteen states to give a clearer picture of the circumstances surrounding violent death. For instance, it looks at the health and economic status of people who commit suicide in order to figure out where to concentrate prevention efforts.

Plant Pathologist

Scientists who study dead plants and trees are called plant pathologists. They are interested in diseases caused by living organisms, like fungi, bacteria, viruses, and parasites. They study these organisms in order to find ways to kill the organisms or manage them by making a plant or tree resistant or changing the environment in which they grow.

They also study environmental factors that cause plant death. These include air pollution, soil nutrient imbalances, water pollution, and the use of pesticides and chemicals. New diseases, evolving organisms, and new ways we pollute our environment are constant threats to our forests, the plants we eat, the plants we use for clothing, like cotton and bamboo, and our beloved landscape plants.

Plant pathologists are employed by colleges and universities, state and federal government agencies, corporations, and nonprofits, like conservation or pollution-control organizations.

Extinction: The Ultimate Death

Extinction is a sad part of life on planet Earth. It happens when the last member of a species of plant, animal, or microorganism dies. This type of species death happens all the time and usually occurs when there is a change in climate which leads to a change in habitat. Most extinctions took place before humans ever walked on the earth. It is estimated that over 99 percent of all species that ever existed are now extinct. Once a species is gone, there's no way to bring it back. Besides becoming a paleontologist, there are other career options if you are interested in studying extinction.

Taxonomists define groups of biological organisms based on their shared characteristics and give names to them. In the past 250 years, taxonomists have named about 1.78 million species of animals, plants, and microorganisms. The total number of species yet to be discovered is unknown, but it is estimated to be between five and thirty million. They also give names to species that have gone extinct but are discovered through the work of paleontologists. For these scientists, extinction means never knowing something existed and not being able to give it a name.

Phylogeneticists study how groups of organisms are related to each other. They study DNA and place each organism on an evolutionary timeline—this organism evolved before or after that organism. Extinct species leave holes in their timeline. These scientists understand how important it is to record the existence of a species before it goes extinct.

Systematists study the changes that take place in living things over time and their relationship to one another. Their work is seen whenever you look at an evolutionary tree. For them too, extinction leaves holes in their data.

The Five Worst Mass Extinctions
Although the extinction of species happens regularly, mass extinctions have only occurred five times over the history of our planet. A mass extinction is when a huge number of species die off.

1. **The Ordovician–Silurian extinction** happened about 439 million years ago when sea levels dropped as glaciers formed, and then rose as they melted. Mostly marine life was affected.

2. **The Late Devonian extinction** happened about 364 million years ago. The cause is unknown, but it appears that warm-water marine life was affected the most.

3. **The Permian–Triassic extinction** happened about 251 million years ago and was the earth's worst mass extinction. It is estimated that 95 percent of all species, 53 percent of marine life, and 70 percent of land species including plants, animals, and insects died. The cause is unknown, but scientists believe either a comet or asteroid hit the earth or a massive volcano erupted.

4. **The End-Triassic extinction** happened about 199 to 214 million years ago. It probably happened when the single continent of Pangaea broke apart, creating the Atlantic Ocean. The eruption and flow of lava caused deadly global warming. Rocks from this eruption have been found in North Africa and Spain as well as the eastern United States and eastern Brazil. About 22 percent of marine life and an unknown percentage of animal life died during this event.

5. **The Cretaceous–Tertiary extinction** happened about sixty-five million years ago. It was probably caused by the impact from a gigantic asteroid that created the Chicxulub crater that is hidden beneath the Gulf of Mexico. Some scientists think this extinction was caused by climate change as a result of volcanic eruptions in central India. About 16 percent of marine life and 18 percent of animal life went extinct, including our beloved dinosaurs.

A Sixth Mass Extinction?

According to Endangered Species International, the sixth mass extinction is happening now. On Earth today, animals are going extinct at a rate that is one hundred to one thousand times faster than the normal rate, which is about ten to twenty-five species a year.

This time, it isn't the fault of a volcano or an asteroid. It is because of human activity. Here are a few of the causes of animal extinction:

- habitat destruction caused by climate change

- habitat destruction caused by invading species

- air, water, and land pollution

- human overpopulation

- overuse of land, over-hunting, and over-fishing

Every continent on Earth is impacted by a loss of diversity among its plants and animals. Since 1500 CE, the start date for recording modern extinct species, the planet has lost 905 species, and 16,938 are considered threatened.

DEAD LANGUAGES

Half of the world's languages are predicted to go extinct in the next hundred years. Currently, about 2,400 languages are dying, with the largest number in India and the United States. A language is considered dead when it is no longer taught to children as a native language. Linguists around the world are trying to preserve dead or dying languages for future generations. This work is important because understanding the definition of words, how they are pronounced, and what they mean to the people who speak or write them is vital to understanding their cultures. The Enduring Voices Project tries to find those languages most at risk for extinction. They document and record the language and work within the community to encourage more native speakers.

R.I.P.

Dead Volcanoes

Volcanologists study volcanoes, and *volcanology* is the scientific study of volcanoes. There are four stages in a volcano's life: erupting, active, dormant, and extinct. Volcanoes are considered dead if they are classified dormant or extinct.

- An **erupting** volcano is currently active and spewing lava, magma, or ash.

- An **active** volcano is one that has erupted since the last ice age, ten thousand years ago, and could again.

- A **dormant** volcano is one that hasn't erupted since the last ice age, but there is a possibility that it will again.

- An **extinct** volcano is one that is no longer expected to erupt.

FIVE DEAD VOLCANOES

- Mount Aconcagua in Argentina is the highest extinct volcano in the world.

- Mounts Terevaka, Poike, and Rano Kau are the three extinct volcanos that formed Easter Island, the most remote inhabited island on Earth.

- Mount Huascarán is the highest extinct volcano in Peru.

- Mount Warning in Australia is the largest and oldest extinct volcano in the world.

- A one-hundred-million-year-old undersea extinct volcano was discovered in August 2014. The gargantuan mountain is in the Pacific Ocean and rises 3,600 feet (1,100 meters) from the sea floor.

If you want to be a volcanologist, major in geology and take courses in related areas like geophysics, sedimentary geology, or geochemistry. With a bachelor's degree, your career is limited to working as an assistant or a technician. If you want to advance in this field, plan to complete a doctorate in geology. As a volcanologist, you will write scientific papers, speak about your work at conferences and scientific meetings, and teach classes. Most volcanologists work 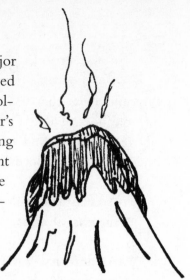 in academia, teaching classes and conducting research during the summer months. Some work for the US Geological Survey (USGS), the government agency responsible for studying the nation's geology, and others work for state governments, especially Alaska, California, Oregon, and Washington, where there is the most volcanic activity.

FRESH MEAT
profile

BRENNA A. HALVERSON, GEOLOGY STUDENT
UNIVERSITY OF HAWAII, HILO
CHEKSHANI CLIFFS, NEW HARMONY, UT
AGE: 19

When did you first discover an interest in volcanoes?
I have always been fascinated by things to do with the earth. I vividly remember when my parents took me with them to Hawaii for a dental conference. I was six. We were able to go out to an active lava flow. I was able to stand about five feet away as it flowed toward us, then right past us. That was probably when I first fell in love with them.

Where are you in your studies? When and how did you decide that studying volcanoes would be your career choice?

Right now, I am in my last year of college. I am currently in my third semester and plan to graduate in the fall of 2015. I hope I will graduate *in absentia*, during my study abroad in New Zealand.

I just grew to love volcanoes. I was in the sixth grade when I really started looking hard at geology as a career. I suppose my love of volcanoes just took off from there. I love learning about how things work and move. Volcanoes are the moving, living, heart of the earth here at the surface.

What is it about volcanoes that fascinates you?

Volcanoes represent the life of the earth. I love living things, and the volcanoes are the "living" part of geology. They breathe. They swell and contract. They grow. They are born and they die. To me, they are living things, not quite in the same sense as animals, but as far as geology is concerned, they are the living, breathing creatures of geology. They are gorgeous, amazing things and just seem to fascinate me.

If you could study a volcano anywhere on Earth, which one would you choose?

Etna (Italy), Stromboli (Italy), and Anak Krakatau (Sumatra) have always fascinated me. Although, honestly, I'd be honored and excited to work on any volcano!! Ngauruhoe in New Zealand is another really interesting one I'd love to work on!

Where do you see yourself in ten years?

I'd love to be working with either the USGS or GNS Science in New Zealand, monitoring volcanoes or doing anything else that has to do with volcanoes. To give you an idea, there is a job opening up via the USGS for either a) a geologist or geophysicist, or b) a geophysicist specializing in volcanic seismology.

This person will be part of a team trying to develop eruption forecasting information systems. That sounds fantastic!

I would also love to get my hands dirty in the field with a specific volcano, knowing its ins and outs and trying to learn more about it, while monitoring it and trying to predict any eruptions, etc. Research would also be awesome! I'd love to be able to research a few odd phenomena in the volcanology world, such as hotspots or why or how a certain cider cone on Mauna Kea formed the way it did. Or maybe work on a pet project of mine from last year, trying to figure out eruption dynamics and how pyroclastic flows move and their deposition process.

Dead Stars

A dead star is one that has stopped creating nuclear fusion. After stars die, they leave remnants behind. They include white dwarfs, which are what's left of a star's core; neutron stars, which are very small, very dense objects of closely packed neutrons; or black holes, which are extremely dense objects with extreme gravitational pull. A black hole's pull is so strong that even light gets trapped inside.

So, why study dead stars? Because they tell us about the history of the universe. They tell us how planets are formed and what happens to them when stars, like our sun, die. But don't worry; our sun isn't expected to die for another five billion years, give or take. When it does, it will become a supernova, creating one of the largest explosions in space. Besides dead stars, scientists look for supernovas in space so they can study the process of star death.

Astronomers study dead stars—and the normal ones too. If you want a job studying the dead in space, this is the job for you. To become an astronomer, plan on going to school long enough to get a doctoral degree in astronomy. Some of the courses you will need are advanced mathematics, engineering, and physics, as well as excellent computer skills. Astronomers work with huge numbers when they work on simulations, calculate distances, or design new instruments. Take note: learn to work on a UNIX-based computer system rather than a Windows-based system early in your studies. It will make your postgraduate work much easier.

About half of all astronomers work as professors at universities and colleges or in the observatories or laboratories associated with them. The rest work for the federal government or at a federally funded national observatory or laboratory. About 10 percent work for businesses or for private institutions, like science museums and planetariums.

STELLAR DIAMOND IN SPACE

Astronomers have found a white dwarf that they think is the coldest one ever detected. It is so cold that the carbon has crystallized, making it an Earth-sized diamond in space. Try wearing that on your ring finger!

FRESH MEAT profile

KATHRYN GRAY AND NATHAN GRAY
WEST KINGS HIGH SCHOOL AND PINE RIDGE MIDDLE
SCHOOL (RESPECTIVELY)
KINGS COUNTY, NOVA SCOTIA, CANADA
AGES: 13 AND 10 (RESPECTIVELY)

When did you first discover a love for astronomy and want to search for supernovas?
Kathryn: Since I was young I've loved to look at the stars. Dad would often bring his telescope along, and we would camp with other astronomers. In 2009, I heard about a girl

named Caroline Moore, who was 14 years old and had discovered a supernova. I thought if she could find one, then I could find one too. I saw my dad find one, and it did not look that hard.

Nathan: Like Kathryn, I remember Dad showing us the night sky with his telescope and thinking it was cool. I wanted to start looking for supernovas when Kathryn found hers! I saw all the fun interviews she got to do and people she got to meet.

How do you search for a supernova? Describe what you do, how often you do it, and how long it takes.

A family friend, Dave Lane, takes pictures on clear nights and sends us the images through the internet. Usually he sends between 100 and 200 pictures. These pictures are of the galaxies that we monitor and take images of over and over again.

We use a computer program called the Supernova Search. This tool allows us to blink [compare] a new picture of a galaxy with an older picture of the same galaxy. We look for a star that appears on the new picture but is not on the old one. As we do the comparison, the new star would appear to blink on and off as all the other stars and the galaxy remain stagnant, or on.

When you find something interesting in one of the photographs, what happens next?

If we find any suspects—potential supernovas—we make notes of them until we are done blinking all of our pictures. Then we call our Dad. He helps us look at the object and determine if we should ask Dave to take another picture of that galaxy. This third picture confirms whether or not the object is still there. If it has moved, it may have been an asteroid. If it is still there, then it is very likely a supernova. If it is still there, we take many new pictures of the suspect. Dad and Dave write an email with all the important information in it and send it to the International Astronomical Union (IAU).

How long does it take scientists to confirm your discoveries?
Kathryn: Sometimes it only takes days. Mine was the next day but Nathan's took three weeks!

Who gets to name your supernovas? How do they choose a name?
We don't get to name them. The IAU has a system of naming them using the year they were found and then a letter for the order they were found. For example, the first one found in 2014 is SN 2014A, the next would be SN 2014B, and so on.

What did they name your supernovas?
Nathan: Mine is called SN 2013hc. It was found in the PGC 61330 galaxy in the constellation Draco (the dragon).
Kathryn: Mine is called SN 2010lt. It was found in the UGC 3378 galaxy in the constellation Camelopardalis.

Besides searching for supernovas, what else fascinates you about space?
Kathryn: I enjoy looking for constellations and like watching the aurora borealis, or Northern Lights.
Nathan: I really like going out and looking up at the sky and scanning with my binoculars to see the Milky Way better.

Where do you see yourself in ten years?
Kathryn: I do not know . . . that is a long time!
Nathan: I want to own my own toy store.

Communicating with the Dead

Psychic and Medium

A psychic is a person who claims to be able to see into the past, know what people are thinking now, and predict the future by tuning in to the energy of a person or object. A medium goes one step further and uses psychic abilities to talk to the dead and help the dead communicate with the living. All psychics are not mediums, but all mediums are psychics.

Psychic detectives work with law enforcement to solve crimes and help find dead victims. Psychic archaeologists use their psychic abilities to find archaeological sites and help others understand the story behind artifacts. Although the scientific community doesn't believe in psychics, there are many people who earn a living using their powers of extrasensory perception. Beyond a psychic sense, to succeed in this field, you must have all the knowledge necessary to successfully run your own business including time management, business, marketing, communication, and financial skills.

DEATH CAFÉS

Death Cafés are where people gather to talk about death. It is a worldwide movement, with almost nine hundred cafés popping up in the past few years. There were over forty in the United States in 2013. Similar to the "café mortel" movement in Switzerland and France at the beginning of the century, these cafés do not offer grief counseling or grief support. The purpose is to provide a safe and comfortable environment to talk about death and the uncertainties in life. People are not allowed to sell products or promote themselves or a particular religion. It's all about conversations, questions, and learning what other people think.

Professional Ghost Hunter

Hunting for ghosts can be scary. Professional ghost hunters are usually called in when an area or a building is reported to have paranormal activity. What you see in the movies or on television is not what life is like for your average ghost hunter. The men and women who work in this field take their jobs and their personal safety seriously. They work in teams, collect evidence, interview witnesses, and investigate the history of the site. Some ghost hunters call themselves paranormal investigators, but since there is no scientific evidence of the existence of ghosts, it is still seen as a pseudoscience.

Ghost hunters use a variety of tools to investigate supernatural activity. Here is a list of some of the most common:

- audio and video recording equipment

- cameras for digital, night vision, infrared, or thermal imaging

- EMF meter to detect changes in electromagnetic fields

- infrared temperature and motion sensors

- ion meter to detect negative ions

Rules for Ghost Hunters

- Never hunt alone.

- Never put your team in danger.

- Be respectful to the spirits.

- Always ask permission before going into an area or building.

- Learn how to speak to ghosts and ask the right questions.

- Know when and when not to provoke a spirit.

- Never use a Ouija board.

- Do your homework—know as much as possible about a spirit before you begin your investigation.

Professional ghost hunters demand that the evidence speak for itself. They do not condone making up stories or faking evidence. Their hope is that one day, the weight of evidence will prove the existence of ghosts.

A professional ghost hunter never charges a client for an investigation. The most any ghost hunter should request is reimbursement for travel expenses. Ghost hunting may be fascinating, especially if you're interested in finding evidence that supports the existence of ghosts, but it's not a path that leads to fame and riches for most.

Famous Ghost Trivia Quiz

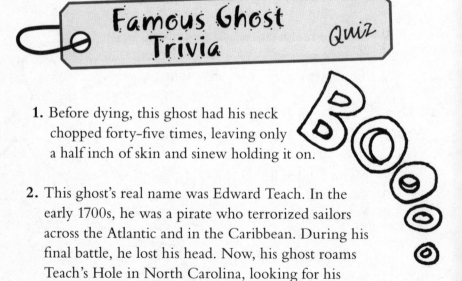

1. Before dying, this ghost had his neck chopped forty-five times, leaving only a half inch of skin and sinew holding it on.

2. This ghost's real name was Edward Teach. In the early 1700s, he was a pirate who terrorized sailors across the Atlantic and in the Caribbean. During his final battle, he lost his head. Now, his ghost roams Teach's Hole in North Carolina, looking for his severed head.

3. This ghost first appeared in comic books in 1945, but it wasn't until 1949 that he received the name we know him by today.

4. According to the doctor who adopted this ghost as a pet, he would "eat anything that's not nailed down or on fire." He is also afraid of broccoli.

5. This ghost is doomed to sail the seas forever! You can see it if you look into the eye of a storm off the coast of the Cape of Good Hope. Beware! If you see this ghost, you will die a terrible death.

6. This ghost was born in 1972, when General Mills introduced the first blueberry-flavored cereal to the American market.

7. These four ghosts appeared in Japan on May 22, 1980. They were the original enemies of Pac-Man and haunted his maze hoping to devour him.

8. According to legend, this ghost haunted the John Bell family for about fifty years in the late 1700s and early 1800s. They lived on a farm on the Red River in Robertson County, Tennessee. Andrew Jackson, before he was president of the United States, met this ghost while traveling through the area.

9. These three ghosts were introduced on December 19, 1843, in a novella by Charles Dickens.

10. This ghost was a freelance "bio-exorcist." He was hired by Barbara and Adam Maitland, a dead couple, to scare away the current, living occupants of their house.

Answers:
1. Nearly Headless Nick from the Harry Potter book series
2. Blackbeard's ghost
3. Casper the Friendly Ghost
4. Slimer from the *Ghostbuster* movies and TV show
5. The Flying Dutchman—a ghost ship
6. Boo Berry
7. Blinky (red), Pinky (pink), Inky (blue), and Clyde (orange) from the Pac-Man arcade game
8. The Bell Witch
9. The Ghost of Christmas Past, the Ghost of Christmas Present, and the Ghost of Christmas Yet to Come
10. Beetlejuice

DEAD LETTERS

The United States Post Office has two dead letter offices, now called *mail recovery centers*. They are located in Atlanta, Georgia, and St. Paul, Minnesota.

The office was created in 1825 to handle mail that couldn't be delivered for a variety of reasons. Workers in mail recovery centers try to reunite pieces of mail with their legal owners. In about 40 percent of the cases, this happens. Once a package or letter is deemed undeliverable, the documents are destroyed, and anything of value in a package is sold at auction.

At the beginning of the twentieth century, the dead letter office received about seven million dead letters a year. Today, the mail recovery centers handle between ninety and one hundred million pieces of mail a year.

11

Industry Resources

Resources for Archaeologists and Paleontologists

Archaeological Institute of America, archaeological.org

The Archaeology Channel, archaeologychannel.org

Archaeology magazine, archaeology.org

Archaeology news, archaeologica.org

Current World Archaeology, world-archaeology.com

The Explorers Club, explorers.org

Paleontological Research Institution and its Museum of the Earth, museumoftheearth.org

The Paleontological Society, paleosoc.org

The Paleontology Portal, paleoportal.org

Passport in Time with the US Forest Service, passportintime.com

Past Horizons, pasthorizonspr.com

Popular Archaeology, popular-archaeology.com

Raymond M. Alf Museum of Paleontology, alfmuseum.org

Society for Historical Archaeology, sha.org

University of Michigan Museum of Paleontology, lsa.umich.edu
/paleontology

Archaeology and Paleontology Websites and Books for Kids

American Archaeology Uncovers the Earliest English Colonies by Lois
Miner Huey

American Museum of Natural History, amnh.org/explore/ology
/archaeology

Archaeology Detectives by Simon Adams

*Archaeology for Kids: Uncovering the Mysteries of Our Past, 25
Activities* by Richard Panchyk

*At Home in Her Tomb: Lady Dai and the Ancient Chinese Treasures of
Mawangdui* by Christine Liu-Perkins

Dig: The Magazine Where History and Archaeology Meet,
digonsite.com

Dinosaurs for Kids, kidsdinos.com

Dinosaurs: The Most Complete, Up-to-Date Encyclopedia for Dinosaur Lovers of All Ages by Dr. Thomas R. Holtz Jr. and Luis V. Rey

DK Eyewitness Books: Fossil by Paul Taylor

National Geographic Investigates Series: Ancient Greece (Ancient Celts, Ancient Iraq, Ancient Maya, etc…)

National Geographic Kids Ultimate Dinopedia: The Most Complete Dinosaur Reference Ever by Don Lessem, Franco Tempesta, and Rodolfo Coria

National Park Service: Kids in Parks, nps.gov/kids

Paleontology: The Study of Prehistoric Life by Susan Heinrichs Gray

Written in Bone: Buried Lives of Jamestown and Colonial Maryland by Sally M. Walker

Young Archaeologists' Club, yac-uk.org

Resources for Funeral Directors

Funeral Directors Associations in each state

Funeral Directors: Job Hunting; A Practical Manual for Job-Hunters and Career-Changers by Stephen Gladwell

How to Land a Top-Paying Funeral Director Job: Your Complete Guide to Opportunities, Resumes and Cover Letters, Interviews, Salaries, Promotions, What to Expect From Recruiters and More! by Brad Andrews

The International Conference of Funeral Service Examining Boards: information on exams, accredited schools, and links to regulatory agencies in each state, theconferenceonline.org

A list of funeral service associations at http://nfda.org/about -funeral-service-/funeral-service-associations.html

National Funeral Directors Association, nfda.org

To Serve the Living: Funeral Directors and the African American Way of Death by Suzanne E. Smith

Funeral Services Books for Kids

Corpses, Coffins, and Crypts: A History of Burial by Penny Colman

Rest in Peace: A History of American Cemeteries by Meg Greene

Resources for Coroners and Medical Examiners

Coroner's Journal: Forensics and the Art of Stalking Death by Louis Cataldie

Coroner's or medical examiner's offices and websites in most counties

Dissecting Death: Secrets of a Medical Examiner by Frederick Zugibe, MD, and David L. Carroll

International Association of Coroners and Medical Examiners, theiacme.com

National Registry of Certified Medical Examiners, nationalregistry.fmcsa.dot.gov/NRPublicUI/MedExAssist.seam

Stiff: The Curious Lives of Human Cadavers by Mary Roach

Working Stiff: Two Years, 262 Bodies, and the Making of a Medical Examiner by Judy Melinek, MD, and T. J. Mitchell

Resources for Forensic Scientists and Entomologists

All about Forensic Science, all-about-forensic-science.com

Amateur Entomologists' Society, www.amentsoc.org

American Academy of Forensic Sciences, aafs.org

American Society of Crime Laboratory Directors, ascld.org

Death Investigation: A Guide for the Forensic Crime Scene Investigator edited by Jeffrey Jones

ForensicED: Forensic Science Education, www.forensiced.org

Forensic Entomology, forensic-entomology.com

Forensic Entomology: An Introduction by Dorothy Gennard

Forensic Entomology: The Utility of Arthropods in Legal Investigations edited by Jason H. Byrd and James L. Castner

The Illustrated World Encyclopedia of Insects by Martin Walters

The International Association of Forensic Toxicologists, tiaft.org

National Forensic Science Technology Center, nfstc.org

North American Forensic Entomology Association, nafea.net

Northwest Association of Forensic Scientists, nwafs.org

The Science of Forensic Entomology by David B. Rivers and Gregory A. Dahlem

Science Spot's Kid Zone, sciencespot.net/Pages/kdzforsci.html

Southern Association of Forensic Scientists, southernforensic.org

US Fish and Wildlife Service Forensics Laboratory: The only crime lab in the world dedicated entirely to wildlife. It serves both the national and international forensic communities, fws.gov/lab

Bug Sites and Books for Kids

Amateur Entomologists' Society: The Bug Club, www.amentsoc .org/bug-club

Bed Bugs: Insect Collecting and Information for Kids, bedbugs .org/insect-collecting-for-kids

BugCollectors.com: How to Collect and Display Insects, bugcollectors.com

Bug Facts, bugfacts.net

Everything Bug: What Kids Really Want to Know about Insects and Spiders by Cherie Winner

The Insect Book: A Basic Guide to the Collection and Care of Common Insects for Young Children by Connie Zakowski

What's That Bug?, whatsthatbug.com

Resources for Historians and Genealogists

American Historical Association, historians.org

American Society of Genealogists, fasg.org

Association of Ancient Historians, associationofancienthistorians
.org

Association of Personal Historians, personalhistorians.org

Becoming Historians edited by James M. Banner Jr. and John R.
Gillis

Family Tree Magazine, familytreemagazine.com

Historians on History edited by John Tosh

*The Information-Literate Historian: A Guide to Research for History
Students* by Jenny L. Presnell

International Society of Genetic Genealogy, isogg.org

The Landscape of History: How Historians Map the Past by John
Lewis Gaddis

National Archives: Resources for Genealogists, archives.gov
/research/genealogy

Organization of American Historians, oah.org

The Pursuit of History by John Tosh

Smithsonian, si.edu/Kids

US Department of State: Office of the Historian, history.state.gov

The USGenWeb Project, usgenweb.org

Resources for Taxidermists

Home Taxidermy for Pleasure and Profit (Illustrated Edition) by Albert B. Farnham

National Taxidermists Association, nationaltaxidermists.com

Taxidermy by Alexis Turner

Taxidermy Art: A Rogue's Guide to the Work, the Culture, and How to Do It Yourself by Robert Marbury

Taxidermy Today, taxidermytoday.com

Taxidermy.net

Resources for the Other Dead Jobs

American Association of Anatomists, anatomy.org

American Association of Clinical Anatomists, clinical-anatomy.org

American Society of Embalmers, amsocembalmers.org

Association for Death Education and Counseling: The Thanatology Association, adec.org

Cremation Resource, cremationresource.org

Cryonics Institute, cryonics.org

The Dead Beat: Lost Souls, Lucky Stiffs, and the Perverse Pleasures of Obituaries by Marilyn Johnson

Extinction Studies Working Group, extinctionstudies.org

The Internet Cremation Society, cremation.org

Kids4Research, kids4research.org

National Association of Government Archives & Records Administrators, nagara.org

National Farmers Organization, nfo.org

Society of American Archivists, www2.archivists.org

12

glossary

anatomy. (uh-nat-uh-mee) A branch of biology that studies the form and structure of organisms.

anthropology. (an-thruh-pol-o-jee) The study of humans, including their origins, culture, environment, and relationships from prehistory to today.

archaeology. (ark-ee-ol-o-jee) The study of past humans, including their origins, culture, environment, and relationships, usually through the fossil record.

ashing. (ash-ing) To burn until only ash remains, then testing to measure the amount of undesirable waste products in a specimen.

atom. (a-tm) The smallest component of an element; it consists of a nucleus, neutrons, protons, and one or more electrons bound to the nucleus by electrical attraction. The number of protons determines the identity of the element.

bioarchaeologist. (bahy-o-ahr-kee-ol-o-jist) A person who studies osteology and uses this knowledge to study human bones found at archaeological sites.

biodegradable. (bahy-o-di-grey-a-bl) Able to decay or break down through the action of living organisms.

botanist. (bot-a-nist) A person who studies plants.

carrion. (kayr-ee-uhn) Dead or rotting flesh.

Celsius. (sel-see-us) Also centigrade—a temperature scale where water freezes at zero degrees and turns to a gas at one hundred degrees.

cerebral. (ser-ree-brul) Involving the brain or intelligence.

clone. (klohn) To create a genetically identical copy of a living organism.

cosmetology. (koz-mi-tol-uh-jee) The art and study of applying makeup.

cremains. (kree-mayns) The cremated remains of a human or animal.

crematory. (cree-muh-tor-ee) The place where cremations take place.

cryobiologist. (krahy-oh-bahy-ol-uh-jist) A person who studies the effects of very low temperatures on living organisms and biological systems.

cryogenicist. (krahy-uh-jen-uh-sist) A person who studies things that have been subjected to extreme cold.

cryonics. (krahy-on-iks) Freezing people after death in the hopes of reviving them later.

cryopreserved. (krahy-o-pree-servd) To preserve something using extremely low temperatures.

curator. (kyoor-ay-ter) A person who cares for something of great value.

decomposition. (dee-kom-po-sish-uhn) The process of decay.

dendrochronology. (den-droh-kruh-nol-uh-jee)
The study of the annual rings of trees to determine
dates and chronological order of past events.

dissect. (dahy-sekt) To cut apart and examine.

DNA. Deoxyribonucleic acid (dee-ox-ee-rahy-boh-noo-klay-ik
as-id), the molecular basis for heredity.

electron. (ee-lek-tron) A particle of matter that has a negative
charge.

entomology. (en-tuh-mol-uh-jee) The study of insects.

excavation. (ex-kuh-vay-shun) The process of digging a hole, to
dig out or remove.

Fahrenheit. (fayr-un-hahyt) A temperature scale where water
freezes at 32 degrees and turns to a gas at 212 degrees.

feller buncher. (fel-er bunch-er) A motorized vehicle with an
attachment that can rapidly cut and gather several trees at a time.

formaldehyde. (form-al-duh-hahyd) A colorless, very smelly gas
used to disinfect and preserve.

genealogy. (jee-nee-ol-uh-jee) The study of a family's ancestors
and history.

geology. (jee-ol-uh-jee) The study of the earth, including its
origin, what it's made of, and how it is changing over time.

glutaraldehyde. (gloo-tuh-ral-duh-hahyd) A chemical used in
tanning leather.

hieroglyphs. (hahy-ro-glifs) A writing system that uses mainly
picture-type characters.

ichnology. (ik-nol-uh-jee) The study of fossilized tracks, trails,
footprints, and other fossil evidence as they relate to the behaviors
of the creature that made them.

isotope. (ahy-suh-tope) Any of two or more forms of the same element that contain equal numbers of protons but different numbers of neutrons in their nuclei; thus, they have different atomic mass or mass number and different physical properties.

linguistics. (ling-gwis-tiks) The scientific study of languages.

macabre. (muh-kob) To have death as the subject, to dwell on the gruesome.

micropaleontology. (mahy-kroh-pey-lee-uhn-tol-uh-jee) The study of microscopic fossils.

mortician. (mawr-tish-uhn) Another name for a funeral director.

mortuary. (mawr-choo-ayr-ee) Relating to the burial of the dead.

neutron. (noo-tron) A particle of matter without a positive or negative charge.

obituary. (o-bi-choo-ayr-ee) A written notice of a person's death that includes some biographical information.

osteology. (os-tee-ol-uh-jee) The scientific study of bones.

paleoanthropology. (pey-lee-oh-an-thruh-pol-uh-jee) The study of prehistoric human fossils, like petrified bones or fossil footprints.

paleobotany. (pey-lee-oh-bot-nee) The study of prehistoric plant fossils.

paleontology. (pey-lee-uhn-tol-uh-jee) The scientific study of prehistoric life using the fossil record.

Pangea. (pan-jee-uh) The landmass that scientists think existed when all the continents were joined, from about three hundred million to two hundred million years ago.

pathology. (puh-thol-uh-jee) The study of the origin, nature, and course of diseases.

petrification. (pet-ri-fi-cay-shun) The process of turning a living organism into rock.

phylogeneticist. (fahy-lo-juh-net-uh-sist) A person who studies how groups of organisms are related to each other, using DNA to place them on the evolutionary timeline.

poltergeist. (pohl-ter-gahyst) A naughty, noisy ghost that is held responsible for unexplained noises.

psychiatrist. (si-kahy-uh-trist) A person who diagnoses and treats mental illness.

psychologist. (sahy-kol-uh-jist) A person who studies human behavior.

radiation. (ray-dee-ay-shun) The process in which energy is emitted as particles or waves.

resuscitate. (ree-sus-i-tate) To try to bring back to life.

rheologist. (ree-ol-uh-jist) A person who studies the distortion and flow of matter.

sedimentary. (sed-i-men-tah-ree) A layer of matter that has settled to the bottom of the ocean or been deposited by wind or glaciers.

sociologist. (soh-see-ol-uh-jist) A person who studies human societies.

synthetic. (sin-thet-ic) Materials created using a chemical process and not from nature.

systematist. (sis-tuh-muh-tist) A person who works to classify and organize organisms.

taphonomy. (tuh-fon-uh-mee) The study of how plants, animals, and humans become fossils.

taxidermist. (tak-si-dur-mist) A person who prepares and preserves the skins of animals and mounts them to look lifelike.

taxonomist. (tak-son-uh-mist). A person who describes, identifies, names, and classifies organisms.

thanatology. (than-uh-tol-uh-jee) The study of death and its surrounding circumstances, as in forensic medicine.

toxicology. (tok-si-kol-uh-jee) The science of dealing with the effects, antidotes, and detection of poisons.

visitation. (viz-i-tay-shun) The time set aside for people to say their final good-bye to someone who has died, usually in a funeral home.

volcanologist. (vol-kuh-nol-uh-jist) A person who studies volcanoes.

wake. (wayk) To stand watch over someone who has died.

zooarchaeology. (zoo-ahr-kee-ol-uh-jee) The study of what remains of animals at an archaeological site, including bones, shells, scales, and DNA.

BIBLIOGRAPHY

Websites

American Association of Anatomists, anatomy.org

American Board of Funeral Service Education, abfse.org

BugCollectors.com, bugcollectors.com

The Encyclopedia of Earth, www.eoearth.org

HowStuffWorks, howstuffworks.com

Interactive Map of Active Volcanoes and Recent Earthquakes World-Wide, earthquakes.volcanodiscovery.com

National Oceanic Service, oceanservice.noaa.gov

National Taxidermists Association, nationaltaxidermists.com

Paleontology Portal, National Science Foundation, paleoportal.org

Professional Association of Ghost Hunters, www.paghosthunters.com

Society for American Archaeology, saa.org

The Society for Paranormal Investigation, paranormalghost.com/index.htm.

The Society of Rheology, rheology.org/sor

Articles, Books, eBooks, and Journals

Academic Invest. "How to Become an Anatomist: Career Path Guide." 2010–2014. http://www.academicinvest.com/science-careers /biology-careers/how-to-become-an-anatomist.

Alford, Justine. "Giant Extinct Volcano Discovered in Pacific Ocean." IFL Science. September 4, 2014. http://www.iflscience.com/environment /giant-extinct-volcano-discovered-pacific-ocean.

AMC.com. "*Immortalized* Handbook: Fun Facts about Taxidermy." *AMC Blog.* January 29, 2013. http://blogs.amctv.com/movie-blog/2013/01 /immortalized-taxidermy-fun-facts/.

American Astronomical Society. "Careers in Astronomy." 2014. http://aas .org/learn/careers-astronomy#work.

American Historical Association. "Careers for History Majors." 2013. http:// www.historians.org/jobs-and-professional-development/career-resources /careers-for-history-majors.

American Museum of Natural History. "Welcome to the Division of Invertebrate Zoology." Accessed July 28, 2013. http://www.amnh.org /our-research/invertebrate-zoology.

American Phytopathological Society. "Careers in Plant Pathology." 2014. http://www.apsnet.org/careers/careersinplantpathology/Pages/default.aspx.

American Phytopathological Society. "What Is Phytopathology or Plant Pathology?" 2014. http://www.apsnet.org/about/Pages /WhatisPhytopathology.aspx.

Antony, Dan. "The Stages of the Human Decomposition Process." GlobalPost. 2014. http://everydaylife.globalpost.com/stages-human -decomposition-process-37600.html.

Art from Ashes. "Frequently Asked Questions." 2006–2014. http://www .artfromashes.com/faq.htm.

Ask an Astronomer. "Curious about Astronomy? Ask an Astronomer." Cornell University Astronomy Department. Last modified May 13, 2011. http://curious.astro.cornell.edu/index.php.

Association for Death Education and Counseling. "About." 2010. http:// www.adec.org/About_ADEC.htm (page discontinued).

Association of Professional Genealogists. "Becoming a Professional Genealogist." 1996–2014. https://www.apgen.org/articles/becoming_a _professional.pdf.

Astroyogi. "Pitru Pashka Do's and Don'ts." Yahoo News. September 19, 2013. https://in.news.yahoo.com/pitru-paksha-don-ts-183012728.html.

Bacon, Lance M. "U.S. Troops Saved Art as the 'Monuments Men' of Iraq." ArmyTimes.com. February 7, 2014. http://www.armytimes.com/article /20140217/NEWS/302170033/U-S-troops-saved-art-Monuments-Men -Iraq.

Banken, CoCo. "The History of Our Monsters." General Mills. October 5, 2012. http://www.blog.generalmills.com/2012/10/the-history-of-our -monsters/#sthash.wes18zWj.dpuf.

Bartlett, Sandra. "Coroners Don't Need Degrees to Determine Death." NPR. February 2, 2011. http://www.npr.org/2011/02/02/133403760 /coroners-dont-need-degrees-to-determine-death.

Berger, Michele. "From Flesh to Bone: The Role of Weather in Body Decomposition." Weather Underground. October 31, 2013. http://www .wunderground.com/news/flesh-bone-what-role-weather-plays-body -decomposition-20131031.

Biles, Jan. "Research Team Starts Cleaning Animal Mounts, Plants at KU Museum." *Topeka Capital-Journal Online*. March 15, 2014. http://cjonline .com/news/local/2014-03-15/research-team-starts-cleaning-animal -mounts-plants-ku-museum.

Bruns, James H. "Remembering the Dead." *EnRoute* 1, no. 3 (July–September 1992). http://www.postalmuseum.si.edu/research/articles-from-enroute/remembering-the-dead.html.

Bryant, Charles W. "How Taxidermy Works." HowStuffWorks.com. February 23, 2009. http://adventure.howstuffworks.com/outdoor-activities/hunting/game-handling/taxidermy.htm.

Bureau of Labor Statistics, US Department of Labor. "Archivists, Curators, and Museum Workers." *Occupational Outlook Handbook, 2014–15 Edition.* Washington, DC: US Department of Labor, 2014. http://www.bls.gov/ooh/education-training-and-library/curators-museum-technicians-and-conservators.htm.

Bureau of Labor Statistics, US Department of Labor. "Epidemiologists." *Occupational Outlook Handbook, 2014–15 Edition.* Washington, DC: US Department of Labor, 2014. http://www.bls.gov/ooh/life-physical-and-social-science/epidemiologists.htm.

California Academy of Sciences. "Collections." 2009. http://research.calacademy.org/ent/collections (site discontinued).

Carlson, K. C. "KC's Bookshelf: Casper the Friendly Ghost 60th Anniversary Special." *Westfield Comics Blog.* 2014. http://www.westfieldcomics.com/blog/interviews-and-columns/kc%E2%80%99s-bookshelf-casper-the-friendly-ghost-60th-anniversary-special/.

Caryl-Sue. "Dia de los muertos." *National Geographic.* 1996–2014. http://education.nationalgeographic.com/education/media/dia-de-los-muertos/?ar_a=1.

CDC/National Center for Health Statistics. "Linked Birth and Infant Death Data." CDC Office of Information Services. Last modified September 24, 2014. http://www.cdc.gov/nchs/linked.htm.

CDC/National Center for Health Statistics. "National Vital Statistics System." CDC Office of Information Services. Last modified December 4, 2014. http://www.cdc.gov/nchs/nvss.htm.

Charney, Noah. "The Real Monuments Men Are Even More Heroic." *Esquire.* February 7, 2014. http://www.esquire.com/blogs/culture/real-monuments-men.

Clark, Liesl. "Mummies 101." *NOVA.* January 20, 1998. http://www.pbs.org/wgbh/nova/ancient/mummies-101.html.

Cohen, K. M., S. C. Finney, P. L. Gibbard, and J. X. Fan. "The ICS International Chronostratigraphic Chart." The International Commission on Stratigraphy. February 2014. http://www.stratigraphy.org/ICSchart/ChronostratChart2014-02.pdf.

The College of Physicians of Philadelphia. "Different Types of Vaccines." The History of Vaccines. Last modified July 31, 2014. http://www.historyofvaccines.org/content/articles/different-types-vaccines.

Cornell University. "How Old Tree Rings and Ancient Wood Are Helping Rewrite History." ScienceDaily. November 2, 2007. http://www .sciencedaily.com/releases/2007/10/071027172611.htm.

"Cornell University Insect Collection." Cornell University College of Agricultural and Life Sciences. 2012. http://cuic.entomology.cornell.edu/.

Cremation Association of North America. "History of Cremation." 2000–2012. http://www.cremationassociation.org/?page=historyofcremation&terms= history.

Cryonics Institute. "Frequently Asked Questions." Accessed August 1, 2014. http://www.cryonics.org/about-us/faqs.

Cultural Resource Analysts. "Paleoethnobotany." 2008–2013. http://crai-ky .com/services/archaeology/paleoethnobotany/.

Cultural Resources, National Park Service, US Department of the Interior. "Federal Historic Preservation Laws: The Official Compilation of U.S. Cultural Heritage Statutes." 2006. National Park Service. http://cr.nps .gov/history/online_books/fhpl/FedLaws_Contents-06.pdf

Daily Mail Reporter. "Actors Fill In at Family Funerals: Chinese Mourners Hiring Professionals to Wail Loudly as Traditional Ritual Dictates." MailOnline. April 6, 2014. http://www.dailymail.co.uk/news/article -2598397/Chinese-mourners-hiring-professional-actors-wail-loudly -traditional-ritual-dictates.html.

DegreeDirectory.org. "What Type of Degree Do I Need to Become a Medical Examiner?" 2003–2014. http://degreedirectory.org/articles/What_Type _of_Degree_Do_I_Need_to_Become_a_Medical_Examiner.html.

Department of Paleobiology, Smithsonian National Museum of Natural History. "Geologic Time: The Story of a Changing Earth." 2014. http:// paleobiology.si.edu/geotime/main/.

"Deputy Coroner I." GovernmentJobs.com. Accessed August 1, 2014. http:// agency.governmentjobs.com/riverside/default.cfm?action=viewclassspec& ClassSpecID=385.

Digital Antiquity. "About." 2013. http://www.digitalantiquity.org/about/.

Dou, Eva. "Roy Rogers' Stuffed Horse Trigger Sold at Auction." USA Today. Last modified July 15, 2010. http://usatoday30.usatoday.com/life /television/news/2010-07-14-roy-rogers-horse_N.htm.

Eastoe, Jane. "11 Historically Important Works of Taxidermy." Mental_Floss. October 11, 2013. http://mentalfloss.com/article/53029/11-historically -important-works-taxidermy.

Economist.com. "Daily Chart: Ashes to Ashes." Last modified November 1, 2012. http://www.economist.com/blogs/graphicdetail/2012/10 /daily-chart-16.

Ectozone. "Slimer." 2014. http://www.ectozone.com/gbfl/slimer.php.

Education Portal. "Coroner: Job Description and Career Info." 2003–2014. http://education-portal.com/articles/Coroner_Job_Description_and _Info_for_Students_Considering_a_Career_as_a_Coroner.html.

Education Portal. "Forensic Morgue Technician: Job Descriptions and Requirements." 2003-2014. http://education-portal.com/articles/Forensic _Morgue_Technician_Job_Descriptions_and_Requirements.html.

Education Portal. "How to Become a Taxidermist: Education and Career Roadmap." 2003–2014. http://education-portal.com/articles/How_to _Become_a_Taxidermist_Education_and_Career_Roadmap.html.

Eduljee, K. E. "Prehistoric Ages." Zoroastrian Heritage. 2005. http://www .heritageinstitute.com/zoroastrianism/reference/ages.htm.

Endangered Species International. "Overview." 2011. http://www .endangeredspeciesinternational.org/overview.html.

Ewing, Rachel. "Drexel Team Unveils *Dreadnoughtus*: A Gigantic, Exceptionally Complete Sauropod Dinosaur." DrexelNow. September 4, 2014. http:// drexel.edu/now/archive/2014/September/Dreadnoughtus-Dinosaur.

Fagan, Brian M. "Chronological Methods 10 - Obsidian Hydration Dating." University of California, Santa Barbara. 1990-1998. http://archserve.id .ucsb.edu/courses/anth/fagan/anth3/Courseware/Chronology/10 _Obsidian_Hydration.html.

Fagan, Brian M. "Chronological Methods 11 - Paleomagnetic and Archaeomagnetic Dating." University of California, Santa Barbara. 1990– 2000. http://archserve.id.ucsb.edu/courses/anth/fagan/anth3/Courseware /Chronology/11_Paleomag_Archaeomag.html.

The Field Museum. "Focus: Insects, Arachnids, and Myriapods." Accessed August 19, 2014. https://www.fieldmuseum.org/science/research/area /focus-insects-arachnids-and-myriapods.

Florida Department of Financial Services. "Examiner Training: Funeral and Cemetery Regulation." 2014. http://fcpr.fsu.edu/funeral/index1.htm.

Fountain, Henry. "Behind the Glass, Primping Up Some Old Friends." *New York Times*. October 21, 2011. http://www.nytimes.com/2011/10/23/arts /artsspecial/diorama-restoration-at-the-american-museum-of-natural -history.html.

Fuller, John. "What Do Bugs Have to Do with Forensic Science?" HowStuffWorks.com. June 18, 2008. http://science.howstuffworks.com /forensic-entomology.htm.

Gaffar, Abdul and Tariq Haqqi. "Immunology—Chapter Fourteen, Immunization." University of South Carolina. July 7, 2010. http:// pathmicro.med.sc.edu/ghaffar/immunization-ver2.htm (site discontinued).

Gannon, Megan. "Cold Dead Star May Be a Giant Diamond." Space.com. June 24, 2014. http://www.space.com/26335-coldest-white-dwarf-star -diamond.html.

Gibb, Timothy J. and Christian Y. Oseto. *How to Make an Awesome Insect Collection: A Beginner's Guide to Finding, Collecting, Mounting, Identifying, and Displaying Insects*. West Lafayette, IN: Purdue Extension, 2011.

Giroux, Amy Larner. "How to Become Certified." Board for Certification of Genealogists. 2007–2014. http://www.bcgcertification.org/certification/index.html.

Gray, Dianne. "Why Facebook Memorials?" Sanctrí. 2013. http://www.sanctri.com/why-facebook-memorials/.

Hadley, Debbie. "Beetles That Eat Bodies." About.com. 2014. http://insects.about.com/od/forensicentomology/tp/Beetles-That-Eat-Bodies.htm.

Hahn, Jeffrey. "Collecting and Preserving Insects." University of Minnesota Extension. 2014. http://www.extension.umn.edu/youth/mn4-H/projects/environment/entomology/collecting-and-preserving-insects/.

Hamphill, Jeffrey. "Radar (Microwave) Remote Sensing." UC Santa Barbara Department of Geography. September 1999. http://www.geog.ucsb.edu/~jeff/115a/remote_sensing/radar/radar1.html.

Hamre, Stian. "Human Osteology." Forensic Osteoarchaeological Services. 2014. http://www.osteoservices.org/html/resources.html.

The Henrietta Lacks Foundation. "About the Henrietta Lacks Foundation." Last modified November 11, 2014. http://henriettalacksfoundation.org/.

Hines, Sandra. "Scientists Find Oldest Dinosaur—or Closest Relative Yet." UW Today. December 4, 2012. http://www.washington.edu/news/2012/12/04/scientists-find-oldest-dinosaur-or-closest-relative-yet/.

Hogg, Jonny. "Madagascar's Dance with the Dead." BBC News. Last modified August 16, 2008. http://news.bbc.co.uk/2/hi/programmes/from _our_own _correspondent/7562898.stm.

Holloway, April. "Turning of the Bones and the Madagascar Dance with the Dead." Ancient Origins. February 15, 2014. http://www.ancient-origins.net/ancient-places-africa/turning-bones-and-madagascar-dance-dead-001346.

Holmes, Susan. "Medicine Man: The Forgotten Museum of Henry Wellcome (1853–1936)." *Journal of Museum Ethnography* 16 (March 2004): 179–181. http://www.jstor.org/stable/40793753.

Hong Kong Tourism Board. "The Hungry Ghost Festival." 2014. http://www.discoverhongkong.com/eng/see-do/events-festivals/chinese-festivals/the-hungry-ghost-festival.jsp.

Howard, Brian Clark. "Pictures: Extinct Species That Could Be Brought Back." *National Geographic*. March 5, 2013. http://news.nationalgeographic.com/news/2013/03/pictures/130305-bring-back-extinct-species/.

Inquisitr. "Rent-a-Mourner Helps You Pad Your Funeral With Weepy, Paid Guests." March 27, 2013. http://www.inquisitr.com/591768/rent-a-mourner-helps-you-pad-your-funeral-with-weepy-paid-guests/.

Institute for Plastination. "The Plastination Process." 2006–2014. http://www.bodyworlds.com/en/plastination/plastination_process.html.

Interdisciplinary Program in Archaeology. "Paleoethnobotany." Washington University in St. Louis. 2014. http://archaeology.artsci.wustl.edu/paleoethnobotany.

Irving Materials, Inc. "What Is Limestone." 2014. https://www.irvmat.com/kids/whatIsLimestone.htm.

Jamison, Peter. "It's a Dog's Afterlife: Pet Death Care Industry Booms." *Tampa Bay Times*. May 2, 2013. http://www.tampabay.com/features/pets/funeral-homes-are-giving-beloved-pets-a-dignified-sendoff/2118135.

Japan-Guide.com. "Obon." 2014. http://www.japan-guide.com/e/e2286.html.

Kelly, Kate. "Embalming Invented During Civil War: How the Civil War Changed Funeral Practices." America Comes Alive. August 3, 2010. http://americacomesalive.com/2010/08/03/wars-drive-advances/#.VFZjRsm-4jo.

Kirby, Doug, Ken Smith, and Mike Wilkens. "Roy Rogers' Horse, Trigger." RoadsideAmerica.com. 1996–2014. http://www.roadsideamerica.com/story/3642.

Klimas, Liz. "4 Million Facebook Users Will Die This Year, and Now There Is a New Way to Honor Their Memory." TheBlaze. November 22, 2013. http://www.theblaze.com/stories/2013/11/22/four-million-facebook-users-will-die-this-year-and-now-there-is-a-new-way-to-honor-their-memory/.

Knight, Bernard. "Crowner: Origins of the Office of Coroner." Brittania.com. 2007. http://www.britannia.com/history/coroner1.html.

Layton, Julia. "How Crime-Scene Clean-Up Works." HowStuffWorks.com. April 6, 2006. http://science.howstuffworks.com/crime-scene-clean-up6.htm.

Lee, James C. "The Undertaker's Role in the American Civil War." June 12, 2006. HistoryNet.com. http://www.historynet.com/the-undertakers-role-during-the-american-civil-war.htm.

Liesowska, Anna. "Exclusive: Siberian Scientists Announce They Now Have a 'High Chance' to Clone the Woolly Mammoth." *Siberian Times*. March 13, 2014. http://siberiantimes.com/science/casestudy/news/exclusive-siberian-scientists-announce-they-now-have-a-high-chance-to-clone-the-extinct-woolly-mammoth/.

Love, Norma. "New in Mortuary Science: Dissolving Bodies with Lye." ABC News. May 8, 2008. http://abcnews.go.com/Technology/story?id=4828249&page=1&singlePage=true.

Maddox, Thomas M., ed. "What You Need to Know about Organ Transplants." WebMD. Last modified July 12, 2012. http://www.webmd.com/a-to-z-guides/organ-transplants-what-you-need-know.

Marius, Maria. "From Lemuralia to All Saints Day." AncientWorlds. Last modified October 25, 2013. http://www.ancientworlds.net/aw/Article /1247491.

Marquis, Erin. "The Driving Dead: Human Cadavers Still Used in Car Crash Testing." AOL Autos. October 24, 2013. http://autos.aol.com/article/the -driving-dead-human-cadavers-still-used-in-car-crash-testing/.

McDonald, Carissa. "10 Festivals That Honor the Dead." Listverse. January 29, 2013. http://listverse.com/2013/01/19/10-festivals-that-honor-the -dead/.

McKone, Harold T. "Embalming: A 'Living' Rite." *Today's Chemists at Work* (December 2002). http://pubs.acs.org/subscribe/archive/tcaw/11/i12/pdf /1202chronicles.pdf.

Media and Public Communications Office of the California Energy Commission. "Chapter 8: Fossil Fuels—Coal, Oil, and Natural Gas." Energy Quest. 1994–2012. http://www.energyquest.ca.gov/story /chapter08.html.

Miller, Stacy. "RNs on the Scene." *Advance*. Last modified March 17, 2014. http://nursing.advanceweb.com/Features/Articles/RNs-on-the-Scene.aspx.

Mooallem, Jon. "The Last Buffalo Hunt: How America's Greatest Taxidermist Helped Save the Bison from Extinction." Slate. May 7, 2013. http://www .slate.com/articles/arts/culturebox/2013/05/william_temple_hornaday _how_a_taxidermist_helped_save_the_buffalo.single.html.

Mullen, Jethro. "Reader Warning: Harvard Experts Say Book Is Bound with Human Skin." CNN. June 5, 2014. http://www.cnn.com/2014/06/05/us /harvard-book-human-skin/.

National Funeral Directors Association. "Exploring a Career in Funeral Service." 2014. http://nfda.org/exploring-a-career-in-funeral-service.html.

National Funeral Directors Association. "NFDA Releases Results of Member General Price List Survey." August 1, 2013. http://nfda.org/news-a-events /all-press-releases/3719-nfda-releases-results-of-member-general-price-list -survey.html.

National Funeral Directors Association. "Statistics." Last modified April 12, 2013. http://nfda.org/about-funeral-service-/trends-and-statistics.html.

National Genealogical Society. "Becoming a Professional Genealogist." 2014. http://www.ngsgenealogy.org/cs/becoming_a_professional_genealogist.

National Geographic. "Prehistoric Time Line." 2014. http://science .nationalgeographic.com/science/prehistoric-world/prehistoric-time-line/.

National Oceanic and Atmospheric Administration. "Marine Archaeologists Use Essentially the Same Excavation Tools as Those Used by Archaeologists Working on Land." Ocean Explorer. Last modified April 2, 2013. http:// oceanexplorer.noaa.gov/facts/marinearch-tools.html.

New Philadelphia Archaeological Project. "Tools Used by Archaeologists." April 28, 2013. http://www.histarch.illinois.edu/np/tools.html.

Ngorongoro Conservation Area Authority. "Oldupai Gorge and Laetoli." 2014. http://www.ngorongorocrater.org/oldupai.html.

Nguyen, Khanh. "Social Epidemiology." University of North Carolina School of Social Work. Accessed July 29, 2014. http://ssw.unc.edu/mch/node/151.

Northampton County Human Resources. "Deputy Coroner." August 2009. http://www.northamptoncounty.org/northampton/lib/northampton /depts/humanresources/DeputyCoronerFTandPT.pdf (site discontinued).

Nuwer, Rachel. "The 'Pompeii of Animals' Shows Dinosaurs, Mammals and Early Birds in Their Death Throes." Smithsonian.com. February 4, 2014. http://www.smithsonianmag.com/science-nature/pompeii-animals-shows -dinosaurs-mammals-and-early-birds-death-throes-180949580/?no-ist.

Occultopedia. "Flying Dutchman." 2014. http://www.occultopedia.com/f /flying_dutchman.htm.

Olsen, Dean. "Coroner System Ancient, but Not Universal in U.S." *Springfield (IL) State-Journal Register*. Last modified May 16, 2010. http:// www.sj-r.com/article/20100516/News/305169946/?Start=1.

Ora, Li. "Professional Obituary Writing." Streetdirectory.com. 2014. http:// www.streetdirectory.com/travel_guide/15775/writing/professional _obituary_writing.html.

Oregon State University. "How Is a Volcano Defined as Being Active, Dormant, or Extinct?" Volcano World. 2014. http://volcano.oregonstate .edu/how-volcano-defined-being-active-dormant-or-extinct.

Owens, Amanda Kate. "A Re-Examination of Cremated Remains from the Archaeological Record: An Evaluation of the Process and Application of Current Methods." Thesis, University of Alabama, 2010. http://acumen.lib .ua.edu/content/u0015/0000001/0000351/u0015_0000001_0000351.pdf.

The Paleontological Society. "The Paleontological Society Code of Fossil Collecting." 2014. http://www.paleosoc.org/pscode.htm.

Peake, Libby. "Dying to Be Green." *Resource*. July 5, 2011. http://www .resource.uk.com/article/Wider_Sustainability/Dying_be_green-1541 #.U81VXbEa2UY.

Pegg, David. "25 Unique and Interesting Ways People Bury Their Dead." List25. June 17, 2013. http://list25.com/25-unique-interesting-ways -people-bury-dead/.

Preston, Douglas. *Dinosaurs in the Attic: An Excursion into the American Museum of Natural History*. New York: St. Martin's Press, 1986.

Rivers, Regina. "Death Midwifery." Rivers Healing Arts. 2009. http:// www.rivershealingarts.com/death_midwifery.php.

Roach, Mary. *Stiff: The Curious Lives of Human Cadavers.* New York: W. W. Norton and Company, 2003.

Rosen, Rebecca. "What Is a Medium?" Oprah.com. May 26, 2010. http://www.oprah.com/spirit/What-is-a-Medium-Rebecca-Rosen.

Rostad, Curtis D. "History of Embalming." Barton Family Funeral Service. 2001. http://bartonfuneral.com/funeral-basics/history-of-embalming/.

Roy Chapman Andrews Society. "Who Was Roy Chapman Andrews." 2014. http://roychapmanandrewssociety.org/roy-chapman-andrews/.

Ruby, Jeff. "This Is What Really Happens during an Autopsy." *Chicago.* April 25, 2013. http://www.chicagomag.com/Chicago-Magazine/May-2013/Bone-Inspector/.

Sachs, Jessica Snyder. *Corpse: Nature, Forensics, and the Struggle to Pinpoint Time of Death.* New York: Basic Books, 2001.

Sahadi, Jeanne. "Six-Figure Jobs: Crime-Scene Cleaner." CNN. April 15, 2005. http://money.cnn.com/2005/02/28/pf/sixfigs_eleven/index.htm.

Schindler, D. and J. Toman. "Convention for the Protection of Cultural Property in the Event of Armed Conflict. The Hague, 14 May 1954." International Community of the Red Cross. 1988. http://www.icrc.org/ihl/INTRO/400.

Schlosser, S. E. "Blackbeard's Ghost: A North Carolina Ghost Story." American Folklore. Last modified December 5, 2014. http://americanfolklore.net/folklore/2010/07/blackbeards_ghost.html.

Schulz, Katja, ed. "Insect Orders." *Encyclopedia of Life.* 2013. http://eol.org/collections/38915.

Science Clarified. "Dating Techniques." 2007–2014. http://www.scienceclarified.com/Co-Di/Dating-Techniques.html.

Science Olympiad. "2014 Entomology (B/C)—Official Insect List." 2014. http://soinc.org/sites/default/files/uploaded_files/OfficialEntomologyList2014.pdf.

Sever, Tom. "Chaco Canyon, New Mexico." Marshall Space Flight Center Earth Science Office. 2014. http://weather.msfc.nasa.gov/archeology/chaco.html.

Shelton, Sally to Conservation DistList. "Cleaning Mounted Birds." November 19, 1996. http://cool.conservation-us.org/byform/mailing-lists/cdl/1996/1168.html.

Shreeve, Jamie. "Species Revival: Should We Bring Back Extinct Animals?" *National Geographic.* March 5, 2013. http://news.nationalgeographic.com/news/2013/03/130305-science-animals-extinct-species-revival-deextinction-debate-tedx/.

Silver, Marc. "A New Chapter in the Immortal Life of Henrietta Lacks." *National Geographic.* August 16, 2013. http://news.nationalgeographic.com

/news/2013/08/130816-henrietta-lacks-immortal-life-hela-cells-genome
-rebecca-skloot-nih/.

Simon Fraser University Museum of Archaeology and Ethnology. "Forensic
Archaeology." Investigating Forensics. 2010. http://www.sfu.museum
/forensics/eng/pg_media-media_pg/archaeologie-archaeology/.

Simon Fraser University Museum of Archaeology and Ethnology. "Forensic
Entomology or the Use of Insects in Death Investigations." Investigating
Forensics. 2010. http://www.sfu.museum/forensics/eng/pg_media-media
_pg/entomologie-entomology/.

Smithsonian Environmental Research Center. "The Lost Colony of Roanoke
Island." Accessed July 12, 2014. http://www.serc.si.edu/education
/resources/watershed/stories/roanoke.aspx.

Smithsonian Museum Conservation Institute. "Conservation Research."
Accessed July 18, 2014. http://www.si.edu/MCI/english/research
/conservation/index.html.

Span, Paula. "Death Be Not Decaffeinated: Over Cup, Groups Face Taboo."
New York Times. June 16, 2013. http://nyti.ms/1aJic7s.

Spitznagel, Eric. "There's Never Been a Better Time to Be a Dead Pet."
Bloomberg Businessweek. September 7, 2012. http://www.businessweek.com
/articles/2012-09-07/theres-never-been-a-better-time-to-be-a-dead-pet
#p1.

Story, Keith. "Approaches to Pest Management in Museums." Presentation at
the Museum Support Center of the Smithsonian Institution, July 24, 1998.
Transcript. http://www.si.edu/MCI/downloads/articles/AtPMiM1998
-Update.pdf.

Struever, Stuart. "Flotation Techniques for the Recovery of Small-Scale
Archaeological Remains." *American Antiquity* 33, no. 3. (July 1968):
353–362. http://www.jstor.org/discover/10.2307/278703?uid=2129&uid=
2&uid=70&uid=4&sid=21104066122471.

Supreme Council of Antiquities Sites. "The Giza Plateau." Accessed July 29,
2014. http://www.sca-egypt.org/eng/SITE_GIZA_MP.htm.

Switek, Brian. "Scientists Discover Oldest Known Dinosaur." Smithsoanian.
com. December 5, 2012. http://www.smithsonianmag.com/science
-nature/scientists-discover-oldest-known-dinosaur-152807497
/#AlIuU3Gr1jBIvMA0.99.

Taxidermy.net. "What Is Taxidermy?" 2005–2006. http://www.taxidermy
.net/information/whatis.html.

Tennessee State Library and Archives. "Bell Witch." 2014. http://www
.tennessee.gov/tsla/exhibits/myth/bellwitch.htm.

Torrance, Megan. "How to Be a Mortuary Cosmetologist." *Houston Chronicle.*
2014. http://work.chron.com/mortuary-cosmetologist-26727.html.

Townsend, Robert. "Historians Defined." Teachinghistory.org. July 7, 2010. http://teachinghistory.org/history-content/ask-a-historian/24120.

TravelChinaGuide. "Qingming Festival (Tomb-Sweeping Day)." 1998–2014. http://www.travelchinaguide.com/essential/holidays/qingming.htm.

Tsolakidou, Stella. "Prehistoric Tablet Calls Into Question History of Writing." Archaeology News Network. July 26, 2012. http://archaeologynewsnetwork.blogspot.com/2012/07/prehistorc-tablet-calls-into-question.html#.U674prEUjIU.

Twyford, Stefani. "Our Top Six Online Memorial Websites." Legacy Multimedia. 2002–2014. http://legacymultimedia.com/2012/03/05/our-top-six-online-memorial-websites/.

United States Postal Service. "Employment Requirements." 2014. http://about.usps.com/careers/employment-requirements.htm.

University of California Museum of Paleontology, Berkley. "The Cambrian Explosion." 1999. http://evolution.berkeley.edu/evosite/evo101/VIIB1c Cambrian.shtml.

US Environmental Protection Agency, Region II. "Burials at Sea." Last modified October 5, 2010. http://www.epa.gov/region2/water/oceans/burials.htm.

USLegal. "Public Vs. Private Cemeteries." 2010–2014. http://cemeteries.uslegal.com/public-vs-private-cemeteries/.

Wagner, Stephen. "The 10 Commandments of Ghost Hunting." About.com. http://paranormal.about.com/od/ghosthuntinggeninfo/tp/10-Commandments-of-Ghost-Hunting.htm.

Wikipedia. "Beetlejuice." 2014. http://en.wikipedia.org/wiki/Beetlejuice.

Wikipedia. "Ghost Hunting." http://en.wikipedia.org/wiki/Ghost_hunting.

Wilkins, Alasdair. "Ancient Poop Science: Inside the Archaeology of Paleofeces." io9. February 9, 2012. http://io9.com/5883873/paleofeces-inside-the-archaeology-of-poop.

Williams, A.R. "Animals Everlasting." National Geographic. November 2009. http://ngm.nationalgeographic.com/2009/11/animal-mummies/williams-text.

Williams, Geoff. "Mysteries of ancient people poop: Vaughn Bryant and Kristin D. Sobolik." Odyssey. March 2008. http://go.galegroup.com/ps/i.do?id=GALE%7CA178452993&v=2.1&u=wccls&it=r&p=ITOF&sw=w&sid=c0d849a19c311ec1ca1d91d360d73d5a

writer873. "Mummification in Ancient Egypt." Ancient History Encyclopedia. January 18, 2012. http://www.ancient.eu.com/article/44/.

Zielinski, Sarah. "Showing Their Age." Smithsonian Magazine, July 2008. http://www.smithsonianmag.com/history/showing-their-age-62874/.

31901059209041